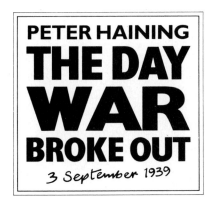

PETER HAINING
THE DAY WAR BROKE OUT
3 September 1939

PETER HAINING

THE DAY WAR BROKE OUT

3 September 1939

W.H. Allen & Co Plc
1989

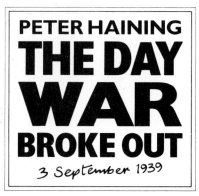

PETER HAINING
THE DAY
WAR
BROKE OUT
3 September 1939

DEDICATION

For my mother and father
who lived through that unique day
and
for my own family
who enjoy life and freedom because of it

First published in 1989 by W.H. Allen & Co. Plc

Typeset by Phoenix Photosetting, Chatham, Kent
Printed and bound in Great Britain
by Mackays of Chatham PLC, Letchworth
for the publishers W.H. Allen & Co. Plc
Sekforde House, 175/9 St. John Street, London EC1V 4LL

Design by Cecil Smith
Cover design by Mike Osborn

British Library Cataloguing in Publication Data

Haining, Peter, *1940–*
   The day war broke out: 3 September 1939
   1. Great Britain, 1936–1945
   I. Title
   941.084

ISBN 1–85227–036–5

WANTED!

FOR MURDER . . . FOR KIDNAPPING . . .

FOR THEFT AND FOR ARSON

Can be recognised full face by habitual scowl. Rarely smiles. Talks rapidly, and when angered screams like a child.

ADOLF HITLER

ALIAS

Adolf Schicklegruber,

Adolf Hittler or Hidler

Last heard of in Berlin, September 3, 1939. Aged fifty, height 5ft. 8½in., dark hair, frequently brushes one lock over left forehead. Blue eyes. Sallow complexion, stout build, weighs about 11st. 3lb. Suffering from acute monomania, with periodic fits of melancholia. Frequently bursts into tears when crossed. Harsh, guttural voice, and has a habit of raising right hand to shoulder level. DANGEROUS!

Profile from a recent photograph. Black moustache. Jowl inclines to fatness. Wide nostrils. Deep-set, menacing eyes.

FOR MURDER Wanted for the murder of over a thousand of his fellow countrymen on the night of the Blood Bath, June 30, 1934. Wanted for the murder of countless political opponents in concentration camps.

He is indicted for the murder of Jews, Germans, Austrians, Czechs, Spaniards and Poles. He is now urgently wanted for homicide against citizens of the British Empire.

Hitler is a gunman who shoots to kill. He acts first and talks afterwards.

No appeals to sentiment can move him. This gangster, surrounded by armed hoodlums, is a natural killer. The reward for his apprehension, dead or alive, is the peace of mankind.

FOR KIDNAPPING Wanted for the kidnapping of Dr. Kurt Schuschnigg, late Chancellor of Austria. Wanted for the kidnapping of Pastor Niemoller, a heroic martyr who was not afraid to put God before Hitler. Wanted for the attempted kidnapping of Dr. Benes, late President of Czechoslovakia. The kidnapping tendencies of this established criminal are marked and violent. The symptoms before an attempt are threats, blackmail and ultimatums. He offers his victims the alternatives of complete surrender or timeless incarceration in the horrors of concentration camps.

FOR THEFT Wanted for the larceny of eighty millions of Czech gold in March, 1939. Wanted for the armed robbery of material resources of the Czech state. Wanted for the stealing of Memelland. Wanted for robbing mankind of peace, of humanity, and for the attempted assault on civilisation itself. This dangerous lunatic masks his raids by spurious appeals to honour, to patriotism and to duty. At the moment when his protestations of peace and friendship are at their most vehement, he is most likely to commit his smash and grab.

His tactics are known and easily recognised. But Europe has already been wrecked and plundered by the depredations of this armed thug who smashes in without scruple.

FOR ARSON Wanted as the incendiary who started the Reichstag fire on the night of February 27, 1933. This crime was the key point, and the starting signal for a series of outrages and brutalities that are unsurpassed in the records of criminal degenerates. As a direct and immediate result of this calculated act of arson, an innocent dupe, Van der Lubbe, was murdered in cold blood. But as an indirect outcome of this carefully-planned offence, Europe itself is ablaze. The fires that this man has kindled cannot be extinguished until he himself is apprehended—dead or alive!

THIS RECKLESS CRIMINAL IS WANTED—DEAD OR ALIVE!

A moment of history: the proclamation of war against Germany being read from the steps of the Royal Exchange in London on 4 September.

*New RAF recruit
T. Sgt 1868811
Haining, William;
and the family
he had to leave at home,
wife Joan and
son Peter.*

R.A.F. Form 2520A
AIRMAN

ROYAL AIR FORCE
SERVICE AND RELEASE BOOK

Rank .... T/SGT ....

Service Number .... 1868811 ....

Surname .... HAINING ....

Initials .... W ....

Class of Release .... A ....

Age and Service Group No. .... 37 ....

51-9768

'Things seemed very quiet and unreal the day war broke out. In fact, they remained so until the actual fighting started in France, to be followed by the Blitz – but that, of course, was long after "the Day".

'It was a perfect Sunday morning and I remember that the air-raid sirens went off and a balloon barrage rose into the air above us. It was actually a quite unnecessary action as no one in Enfield expected any offensive enemy aircraft to appear.

'Briefly, though, four of our own twin-engined Blenheim fighter bombers did a very unmilitary "ballet" over north London, and one can only think it was to show the people on the ground that we had aircraft and were ready to use them. A comic footnote to this occurred at Clay Hill near where we lived. Two elderly people opened their windows and stuck their heads out to see what was going on. Both of them were wearing gas masks!

'The following day, Monday, was also fairly normal in many ways, though I do remember the youngest male members of our staff at the office – about to be called up – saying with dry humour, "Well, at least we are in the final – the Poles, Austrians, Czechs, etc. have all been beaten!"'

William Haining, the author's father

MOTHERS
Send them out of London

Give them a chance of greater safety and health

Hitler will send no warning –
so always carry your gas mask

ISSUED BY THE MINISTRY OF HOME SECURITY

For a healthy, happy job

Join the **WOMEN'S LAND ARMY**

for details
APPLY TO NEAREST W.L.A. COUNTY OFFICE OR TO W.L.A. HEADQUARTERS 6 CHESHAM PLACE LONDON S.W.1 STREET
Issued by the Ministry of Agriculture and the Ministry of Labour and National Service

DIG FOR VICTORY

Contents

THE KING AND HIS PRIME MINISTER OF PEACE

★

A memorable picture of a memorable occasion . . . taken when the Prime Minister, in the hour of his greatest triumph, went with Mrs. Chamberlain to see the King and Queen at Buckingham Palace.

With a happy gesture their Majesties surrendered central place to the man who has worked so unswervingly for peace and to the woman who has been his constant helpmate.

In that moment they symbolised the heartfelt gratitude of the nation—the gratitude that had drawn crowds, despite rain, to wait outside the Palace to see the Prime Minister.

ENGLAND ACCLAIMS THE PREMIER

Surrounded by Cabinet Ministers, Mr. Chamberlain pictured at Heston on his triumphant return from Munich.   Thousands gathered to welcome him.

'Peace for our time' – the hopes of October 1938 when
Prime Minister Neville Chamberlain returned from
Munich with a peace agreement were to be dashed just
a year later. (Daily Sketch, *1 October 1938*)

1 A Balmy September Day

The morning of Sunday 3 September 1939 dawned bright and clear over the British Isles, the sun shining down from sparkling blue skies in what was already the autumn season. In fact, the morning was in many respects like most of those of the previous month which had been one of the warmest and driest on record. It was, however, to prove quite unlike any other – for before the day was over Britain would be at war with Germany for the second time in the twentieth century.

Although the clouds of war had been steadily gathering around the nation that long, hot summer, many people had tried to take advantage of the weather. And putting aside thoughts of Hitler and his dark forces, these Britons had decided that this might well be the last chance they would have for some time – possibly years – for a holiday, and grabbed at the chance.

For those of the United Kingdom's population of 44 million people who could remember the outbreak of the previous war a quarter of a century earlier, both the atmosphere and the weather on this Sunday morning were totally different. Then, the declaration of war had come almost unexpectedly in the night of 4 August 1914 as a result of the German invasion of Belgium – and had been immediately followed by a fog which enveloped all the armies and frontiers involved in the conflict. On the balmy September day when Britain once again found herself lined up against her former enemy, it followed months of protracted negotiations and even one declaration – by the Prime Minister, Neville Chamberlain – that there would be 'peace for our time'.

The distinguished diplomat, writer and (at the time) Liberal MP for West Leicester, Harold Nicolson, who was to be knighted in 1953, perfectly summarized these differences when writing in *The Listener* of 14 September 1939: 'It is essentially a difference between gradualness and urgency. We lolled and slouched into the First German War; the Second has found us infinitely more prepared.' Sir Harold's own fascinating personal memories of these two days appear on page 19.

The origins of the Second World War which drew Britain (and the Commonwealth countries who came to her assistance), France, Russia, China and America into conflict with Nazi Germany, fascist Italy and Japan have, of course, been fully analysed and debated in a whole plethora of books by eminent historians and so require no more than a brief outline in a popular history such as this.

It is generally agreed that the war was sparked by a series of aggressive acts by what became collectively known as the Axis powers: the Japanese first conquering Manchuria in 1931, followed by the Italian conquest of Ethiopia in 1935, the German and Italian

Despite the grimness of the news, a cheerful group of Londoners gathers in Downing Street on the morning of 3 September to await the announcement of war from Number 10.

intervention in the Spanish Civil War (1936–9), the further Japanese invasion of China in 1937, Hitler's annexation of Austria in March 1938, the Sudetenland in September 1938 and Czechoslovakia in March 1939, and yet another Italian conquest, that of Albania, in April 1939.

The response of both Britain and France to these hostile moves was a policy of 'appeasement' which in September 1938 produced the notorious Munich Agreement. However, public reaction in Britain to the annexation of Czechoslovakia six months later compelled both its own government and that of the French to open negotiations with Russia to form a peace bloc against the menace of Germany. These negotiations broke down dramatically in August 1939 when the Russian leader Stalin instead drew up a non-aggression pact with Hitler.

It was the German invasion of Poland on 1 September which finally caused the British Government to issue an ultimatum to the Nazi leader to withdraw his forces 'immediately'. When the deadline for this withdrawal, 11 a.m. on that warm September Sunday, passed with no response from Hitler, Chamberlain was left with no alternative. At 11.15 a.m. he broadcast to the nation from the Cabinet Room of 10 Downing Street, 'Britain is at war with Germany.'

Though there was at that moment a large, hushed audience of Britons gathered around their radios to hear the Prime Minister, others were out of doors: some working in their gardens, others taking walks, a great many more at church. In the main, these folk still clung to the hope that the Government would find some last-minute means of avoiding conflict.

But when, just a few minutes after Chamberlain's speech had ended, sirens began to wail across southern England and the population was forced to seek the protection of air-raid shelters for the very first time, these people – like everyone else – knew that any such hopes had foundered. Although the warning proved a false alarm, the nation as a whole realized that it was about to have to do all over again what it had done in 1914.

On the political front, Chamberlain set about assembling his War Cabinet and made what was to prove one of his finest decisions: appointing Winston Churchill as First Lord of the Admiralty. It was an immensely popular and morale-boosting choice with the people, for Churchill had held the same post with outstanding success twenty-five years earlier in 1914.

Although the Member of Parliament for Epping had been virtually a political exile since 1929, his prestige with the public had never been higher, particularly as through all these years he had repeatedly warned about the growing menace of the Nazis, warnings that had earned him in Germany the title 'Nazi Enemy No. 1'.

Rarely in human history can such an epithet have been so accurately applied and ultimately justified.

The lives of many people in Britain had, however, already been widely disrupted by the dawn of that Sunday morning. The massive evacuation of schoolchildren, mothers and babies from the danger areas of big cities into the countryside was already largely over and many separated families heard the news they had feared from different locations. The preparations for attack had also been organized, and the blackout was already in place in many homes, while gas masks hung ready for use by the front doors, and outside, the air-raid shelters awaited occupation when the bombers came. Over the large cities, huge balloons shaped like silver larvae hung suspended, offering the reassurance of protection from enemy planes.

In the streets, the recently formed bands of Air-Raid Wardens were at last preparing to put their training into practice, while the Army, Navy and RAF began to make plans for the call-up of servicemen between the

ages of eighteen and forty-one – a figure that was to be raised to fifty-one in 1941 when women were also included in conscription (though in fact, no man over forty-five was ever called up).

Amazing as it may seem, only about one-tenth of the population of Great Britain was actually to serve in the armed forces for much of the war. According to the official records, in the autumn of 1939 the number of servicemen registered was 727,000; in 1940 this climbed to its peak of 4,100,000, and then fell to 2,222,000 a year later. After this, the numbers continued to decrease up to the end of the war.

For the one and a half million unemployed people in the country, the declaration of war meant a change of fortune. Those who were not called up might now hope to find employment in the factories and munitions industry – though there was undoubtedly a worry as to where the next meal might be coming from when rationing and austerity began to bite.

The one thing that all Britons were already resolved

THE MOMENT WAR BEGAN

'Diplomatic documents, however dramatically exchanged, do not constitute ocular evidence that war has begun. Street demonstrations and press notices are mass experiences and not individual. It interests me to ascertain what personal experience was the first to convince any given citizen that we had in fact placed ourselves upon a war basis.

'In August 1914, I made a careful note of my own experiences in this respect. The first sign of war that I observed occurred when I was in a train coming up from Kent to London. Somewhere in Lewisham there had long been established some Territorial battery which housed a gun in a shed close to the railway line. There was a patch of grass in front of this shed, and as the train passed close to it I noticed that the grass had been churned up by heavy wheels. I realized that the gun had earlier that morning been taken out of its shed. That was the first ocular demonstration of military action. When I reached London I passed an army lorry in Belgrave Square packed with little ordnance maps. That was my second piece of evidence. And within a few short hours the evidences accumulated so rapidly that they made no further impress on my mind.

'This time my experience was far more dramatic. It was one which was shared by many of my fellow countrymen. Only a few minutes after listening to the Prime Minister's broadcast address on Sunday I walked down with one or two friends to my place of business; and while I was walking through the streets the sirens warbled around us. I was only a very little distance from a place in which, I knew, I should both find refuge and be able to fulfil my functions. The question arose whether, as a most obedient citizen, I should seek refuge immediately in the nearest basement or refuge, or whether, as a conscientious worker, I should defy regulations and make for my place of business. On consideration I decided that my own air-raid refuge would be preferable. My duty as a worker triumphed for this reason over my civic conscience and with hurried although not, I trust, undignified steps, I escaped across Parliament Square.

'That, I think, will for all of us remain the great difference between 1914 and 1939. The First German War was made manifest to me by seeing some grass trampled by the wheel of a Territorial gun; the Second German War intruded itself upon my consciousness owing to the necessity of having to seek shelter rapidly some thirty minutes after war had been declared.'

Harold Nicolson
The Listener, 14 September 1939

---

upon was that life must go on. The circumstances under which they lived might now be very different, and the conditions were certainly going to get worse before they got better; but the British way of life had always been the cornerstone on which its citizens built their society, and no little German dictator was going to put an end to *that*. For such was, and is, the British character – and so it proved in the years which followed that September day when war broke out.

In the pages which follow, the reader will find described the impact and immediate effects of the start of the war on day-to-day life in Britain as well as the way in which it affected the ordinary men, women and children of the country. The war of the statesmen and the soldiers has been fully told; this is the story of the war of the people, or more particularly how they confronted it and prepared for the future. Some writers have called this period the 'Phoney War', and although there was undoubtedly a feeling of anticlimax when the Nazis did not come in planes and boats to ravage the countryside with gas and bullets as some people had predicted, life *did* change profoundly for one and all in a way that no one who was not alive at the time – or has not had actual experience of wartime – can fully appreciate.

A London woman, Patricia Hardy, just turned twenty-one that September and now a white-haired grandmother in her seventies, speaks for the whole nation as it was then when she reminisces about that unique Sunday.

'It was a glorious morning,' she says, 'and Mum, Dad and I were up early listening to every bulletin. When war was declared I had this funny feeling inside me, a sort of mixture of relief, almost elation. When Mr Churchill said, "In our hearts this Sunday morning there is peace" it was certainly true for us. Later in the day when the King made his speech we all three stood to attention.

'I suppose I was surprised that nothing seemed to have altered, now that we were actually at war. I don't think it entered our heads that some of us might get killed. But I know we were all of the same mind that day – that we *must* win.'

I hope that in the pages which follow older readers will be stirred by nostalgic memories of their lives during those days; their children (of which I am one) reminded of what they were too young to remember except in brief flashes; and today's generation appreciate what it was that their grandparents strove so courageously to preserve. For that war which began fifty years ago was as surely won in Britain as it was on any of the far-flung battlefields of the world.

2 Drama in the House

On the day that war was declared Britain became, in effect, a totalitarian state. In a sense, it already *was* one for on 24 August the Emergency Powers (Defence) Bill had been passed by both Houses of Parliament and received the assent of the King. This, quite simply, enabled the Government to introduce whatever regulations it saw fit and in the following week a whole block of over 500 new laws was introduced on to the statute books which placed restrictions on every aspect of public life – even allowing officials unrestricted entry into that most sacred of all an Englishman's preserves: his home.

Beyond any question, these new emergency laws gave the Government quite awesome powers that in the hands of less reasonable people could have led to terrible abuses – which is not to say that there were not the occasional instances of misuse of authority. Parliament could now alter or suspend any Act that it chose. It was now also within the Government's right (or more precisely that of its appointed officials) to seize any piece of property they required, to imprison without trial anyone felt to be a threat to public safety, to impose a curfew at night, to instruct manufacturers what they could build, farmers what they could sow and shopowners what they might sell. And the state's officials now had the right to go where and at what time they chose to ensure that all these regulations were carried out to the letter of the law.

Strangely, only money escaped the draconian laws. For Parliament did not propose to give itself the power to seize gold, currency or securities – although it was decreed that any British citizen who possessed financial holdings abroad was under an obligation to offer these for sale to the Treasury.

The variety and complexity of these new measures – and more were to be added in the days and weeks which followed – not to mention the plain absurdity of some of them, are such that a mere listing of their titles would probably fill the pages of this book. Indeed, an official publication containing those in force by 3 September ran close to 500 pages! Yet there should just be mention of a few of the more unusual examples.

For instance, British stomachs were hit by the law which prevented diners in restaurants from having more than a single choice for their main course, while children were no longer to be allowed sugar on their sweets. Youngsters were also banned from flying kites, and the age-old practice of campanology (bell-ringing) joined the forbidden list. Anyone travelling abroad would now be breaking the law if they did not give up any newspapers or magazines in their possession before leaving the country, and photography came in for the most stringent restrictions as to the kind of places and even the people (mainly military personnel) that could not be snapped. The humble roadside signpost similarly fell under these laws when it was decided that they might give help to spies or enemy agents and must therefore be removed.

Of course, while these new regulations and the day-to-day working of Parliament were being earnestly recorded in the pages of *Hansard* and the columns of the daily newspapers as the country moved from peace into a state of war, another and perhaps far more interesting question remained: what was the atmosphere like in the House of Commons? In particular, how were the elected men and women, charged with representing the millions of their fellow countrymen anxiously awaiting news of their deliberations, faring under the strain? Two reports, both written at the time by MPs, one a Conservative back-bencher, Mr Ralph Glyn, and the other a forceful Labour Member, Mrs Ellen Wilkinson, probably better convey the emotions of MPs at this crucial moment in the nation's history than any official report. They are also of special interest, I believe, because neither has been published in a book before.

First, the account of Berkshire MP Mr Glyn, the Member for Abingdon since 1924. He kept a diary throughout his term as a Member and committed the following thoughts to paper immediately after the declaration.

'*September 3*. Last night in London was one of the great times in modern history. The half-hour in the Commons – 7.30 to 8 – was perhaps the most decisive half-hour that we have known.

'All through the day the House had been in a schoolboyish, almost hysterical mood; they were laughing and shuffling. There was a feeling that something fishy was happening in Downing Street. The Cabinet was still sitting. Ministers were telephoning Paris – and the Germans were bombing Poland. *Why* were we not at war?

'At half-past seven we met again, this time subdued and tense. Chamberlain we knew would declare war. The Ambassadors were looking down; Count Edward

Three MPs prepare for war in the Parliamentary Home Guard. Acting Sergeant Vernon Bartlett (left) gives instruction on how to use a sten gun to Private Sir Geoffrey Shakespeare and Corporal Gordon Touche in the shadow of Big Ben.

Raczijnsky pale and worn. Chamberlain came in looking grey – a kind of whitish-grey – and glum, dour. Captain Margesson, the Secretary to the Treasury, came behind him, purple with anxiety. Chamberlain's statement! . . . In the house we thought he was only half-way through when – he sat down. There was a gasp, first of horror, then anger. His own back-benchers leaned forward to cry, "Munich, Munich!" The House seemed to rise to its feet with Mr Arthur Greenwood, the Labour leader.

'Mr L. S. Amery, sitting very small near Anthony Eden, jumped up to shout at Greenwood – "Speak for England." Others took up the cry. Chamberlain white and hunched. Margesson with sweat pouring down his face, Sir John Simon, the Foreign Secretary, punctiliously looking holy.

'Greenwood spoke slowly and very simply. He spoke for England and what is more he saved Chamberlain by most skilfully suggesting that it was the French who were delaying. Then one or two backbenchers, Chamberlain's own supporters, got up. It was not a joint Anglo-French pledge to Poland, they said, it was a *British* pledge – why were we not fulfilling it? The House swung against Chamberlain again. Winston Churchill, I saw, was getting whiter and grimmer. He turned round to look at Eden, who nodded as if to say, "You speak, I'll follow." I know that Churchill was about to move a vote of censure on the Government – which would have fallen. But Chamberlain looked across at Churchill: "I'm playing straight," his glance seemed to say, "there really *are* reasons for delay." Churchill sat back, relaxed, uneasy.

'Then James Maxton, the pacifist, rose, gaunt, a Horseman from the Apocalypse, doom written across his face: "Don't let's talk of national honour: what do such phrases mean? The plain fact is that war means the slaughter of millions. If the Prime Minister can still maintain the peace he will have saved those lives, he mustn't be rushed." Again the House swung and was poised. We all thought in the curious hush: What if the gaunt figure of doom were right after all? Slaughter – misery – ruin – was he right? But the alternative: Hitler trading on our fears, Germany treading on freedom, Europe under terror. The whole House was swayed in unison with the drama which itself was living.

'Another back-bencher spoke: "We must keep our pledge – Hitler must be stopped." Once again we were swinging against Chamberlain, when Margesson, damp and shapeless, rose to move the adjournment. In a kind of daze it was carried.

'We broke up, some feeling sick from the reaction – two members *were* sick – all were uneasy and ashamed. I went home, lay awake all night, slept a bit towards

morning, and was awakened by the air-raid warning. Had the Germans read the feelings of the country? Were they attacking first?

'From my window I could look over London – it is the clearest and sunniest and freshest day we have had this year. St Paul's dome shone blue, and to the east I could see the smoke and masts of the ships at the wharves all peaceful under a blue sky. Later – at 11.15 – I heard Chamberlain's announcement. We had gone out to meet Hitler, we were at war.'

Ralph Glyn's comments for the following day are also just worth adding.

'*Monday, September 4.* To-day London was in a state of the most complete unreality. Are we at war?

'We have declared war, that is certain, but are we *at* war? The Poles are being driven back; why are we not helping? Is there another game on? One or two of the well-informed still speak of another Munich, even at this late hour. They said Hitler might smash Poland before the war really got going in the West; then he would offer peace; and we should accept. The Poles here are wondering whether the British and French really mean business and *mean it in time*. No one in London is yet convinced that we really are at war and are really going through with it.

'This evening has come the most *macabre* story which I have ever heard. Unfortunately it is true. On the day when the merchant ship, the *Athenia* was torpedoed, when 17 Polish towns were bombed, and when the Poles were being pressed back, we sent a number of RAF machines over Germany and they dropped *leaflets!* No wonder that no one believes in war.'

The report from the other side of the House by Ellen Wilkinson, former union leader and Labour Member for Jarrow since 1935, was not committed to paper until the end of the first week of September, but as a result is able to add some fascinating inside information on the reasons for Chamberlain's vacillations. Mrs Wilkinson's comments on the various new regulations are also, I think, particularly revealing!

'The House of Commons in wartime is giving an

One of the famous series of Punch *cartoons by perhaps the best remembered of all the wartime cartoonists, 'Fougasse' (Kenneth Bird), humorously observing the changes war brought to Britain. (15 September 1939)*

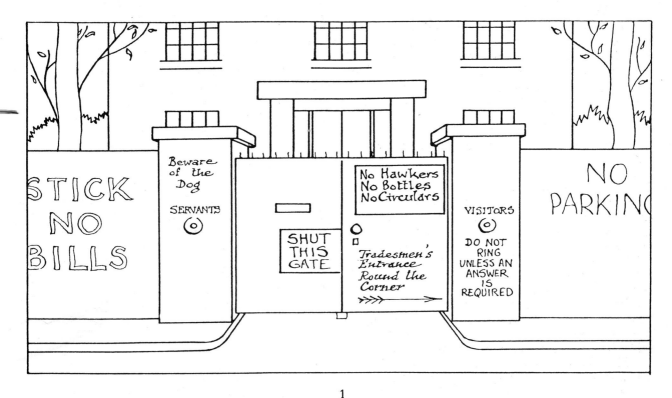

1

2

example of brotherliness and mutual consideration that would be positively alarming if it were not so pleasant. Ancient enemies sit in friendly conference in every corner. Men who were at each other's throats over the Spanish conflict manage to discuss the news quite amicably. One side is uncomfortable about Franco and the other about Stalin, so there is a kind of understood truce for the time being. Not even the war could of itself have produced this effect. It dates from the shock of last Saturday. All day round the crowded House rumours had gone about like wisps of smoke. "The French are not coming in with us." We know now how the rumour started. Général Gamelin, having to move something like five million men, naturally preferred to do it in normal peace. His moving columns could not then be bombed. Besides, he had the appalling task of redrafting his plans, for the original French plan of attack had been revealed to the Russians during the recent military conversations. But we did not know that on Saturday afternoon. The Premier's statement postponed and re-postponed only added to the uneasiness.

'Isolationist MPs had stalked round the House of Commons last September asking scornfully, "Why should we fight for the Czechs anyway?" Now they knew what the Czechs had felt like during the hours of waiting for England's answer. But it was queer how MPs drew together during those hours. When the Premier seemed to justify every rumour by his further postponement he found the House ninety per cent against him – and he knew that if Britain was not brought to the help of Poland on Sunday his government would fall. On Saturday night MPs went home with grim, unhappy faces. Yet the next day, jammed in our air-raid shelter, the war declared, we were happy. The fight to stop aggression had begun.'

Turning to the new regulations being hurried through the House, Mrs Wilkinson went on:

'Not even in 1914 has a Government had such halcyon days, such a legislative honeymoon. Bills have

Once war had been officially declared the people of Britain determined it was to be 'business as usual' – as this photograph of rush-hour workers in the city (complete with gas masks!) taken in London on the morning of 4 September clearly shows.

British women were as quickly involved in the war as men – here a female Air-Raid Warden is seen on duty at her underground post in Westminster.

THE OLD SEA-DOG

" Any telegram for me? "

passed through the Chamber as through a smooth tube. Incidentally, some of the Bills are quite unworkable. There will have to be some sort of Special Commission to sort them out. The Parliamentary draughtsmen are a very small group of men. They have had to work all night doing work that needs fresh, alert minds. Faults can be put right, but what Parliament rightly concerned itself about was the main issues.

'The wife of a man who is called up is now protected from eviction or rent increases. The small man buying a house, the worker suffering from unemployment but not insured are now covered. Other minor tragedies of the war have been foreseen and legal power taken to give help. If the details are not quite right what matters is getting the principle established.

'A Bill to confine workers to their present jobs is more controversial. It is a little early to start on this difficult field. Most people want to be something more thrilling than they are, every ill-paid unskilled worker has visions of good jobs on munition work. But it is not enough to force them to remain without investigation of individual cases.

'Some MPs have been impatient about all this work being done by Parliamentary Bills instead of doing it by regulation. But regulations are not open to criticism. It is important that when Bills affecting the intimate life of every citizen are being rushed through Parliament they should have at least a rapid scrutiny by the elected representatives of those citizens. The House of Commons has done a good job under great difficulties. Left to itself without scrutiny the official mind might have restricted liberties of the ordinary citizen beyond anything that was really necessary in a situation where everyone is ready to be helpful.'

Mrs Wilkinson finally devoted a little space to commenting on the central figures in the drama that was being played out all around her in the House.

'With the intense concentration on the individuals who have to speak to the crowded House at the times when announcements are made, reputations rise or wither quickly in such heat. The House welcomed Mr Churchill as a Minister, so obviously feeling that things might have been very different if he had been in the Cabinet these last two years.

'Sir John Anderson, now Head of the Home Office, has been rather under a cloud. He has tended to bore the House with his long and complicated ARP Bills. But when he made his statement on Britain's attitude to aliens and to refugees he shot up to the top scale. The House as a whole recognized the tolerance and the statesmanship shown in his refusal to vent on innocent refugees the sins of the rulers from whom they had fled.

'Mr Arthur Greenwood has done well. His speeches have expressed what the masses of the people are thinking. At the same time he has been able to voice criticism while making clear the unalterable resolution of his Party to resist aggression. It is difficult to do this without seeming to be hindering national effort at a time of emergency, but he has done it well. . . .

'As one moves about the various departments, any MP doing service for his constituents cannot fail to be heartened by the quality of the work which our Civil Servants are doing. The evacuation has gone like clockwork under the hands of a few young men working night and day. The overwork is terrible but inevitable until Britain settles in to her appalling task. Many civilians who have volunteered to help may feel disgruntled because they are not being used immediately. The thing is to remember that everyone cannot be used at once. In the waiting period, find the nearest job to be done and do it. At least fill a sandbag or help to amuse evacuated children if the call for wider service does not come immediately.'

Mrs Wilkinson's praise for the evacuation of the nation's schoolchildren and its young mothers and babies was certainly deserved – though as closer enquiry and subsequent investigation have shown, there was also another very different side to this first chapter in the story of the day war broke out . . .

'The House welcomed Mr Churchill as a Minister' – a brilliant cartoon by E. H. Shepard of Punch *which reflected the nation's feeling as to the importance of the Epping MP playing a leading role in the conflict to come.*

"BRITAIN IS AT WAR WITH GERMANY"

In a broadcast from Downing Street, at 11.15 a.m. on Sunday, Sept. 3, 1939, the Prime Minister said :—

"THIS morning the British Ambassador in Berlin handed the German Government a final Note stating that unless we heard from them by eleven o'clock that they were prepared at once to withdraw their troops from Poland a state of war would exist between us.

" I have to tell you now that no such undertaking has been received, and that consequently this country is at war with Germany.

" You can imagine what a bitter blow it is to me that all my long struggle to win peace has failed. Yet I cannot believe that there is anything more, or anything different that I could have done and that would have been more successful.

" Up to the very last it would have been quite possible to have arranged a peaceful and honourable settlement between Germany and Poland, but Hitler would not have it.

" He had evidently made up his mind to attack Poland whatever happened, and although he now says he put forward reasonable proposals which were rejected by the Poles, that is not a true statement.

" The proposals were never shown to the Poles, nor to us, and though they were announced in a German broadcast on Thursday night Hitler did not wait to hear comments on them, but ordered his troops to cross the Polish frontier. His action shows convincingly that there is no chance of expecting that this man will ever give up his practice of using force to gain his will. He can only be stopped by force.

" We and France are today, in fulfilment of our obligations, going to the aid of Poland, who is so bravely resisting this wicked and unprovoked attack on her people.

" We have a clear conscience. We have done all that any country could do to establish peace.

" The situation in which no word given by Germany's ruler could be trusted and no people or country could feel themselves safe has become intolerable.

" And now that we have resolved to finish it I know that you will all play your part with calmness and courage.

" At such a moment as this the assurances of support that we have received from the Empire are a source of profound encouragement to us.

" When I have finished speaking certain detailed announcements will be made on behalf of the Government. Give these your closest attention.

" The Government have made plans under which it will be possible to carry on the work of the nation in the days of stress and strain that may be ahead. But these plans need your help.

" You may be taking your part in the fighting services or as a volunteer in one of the branches of civil defence. If so, you will report for duty in accordance with the instructions you have received.

" You may be engaged in work essential to the prosecution of war, for the maintenance of the life of the people—in factories, in transport, in public utility concerns, or in the supply of other necessaries of life.

" If so, it is of vital importance that you should carry on with your jobs.

" Now may God bless you all. May He defend the right. It is the evil things that we shall be fighting against—brute force, bad faith, injustice, oppression and persecution—and against them I am certain that the right will prevail."

The King to His Peoples

Broadcast from Buckingham Palace by H.M. KING GEORGE VI on September 3, 1939

IN this grave hour, perhaps the most fateful in our history, I send to every household of my peoples, both at home and overseas, this message, spoken with the same depth of feeling for each one of you as if I were able to cross your threshold and speak to you myself.

For the second time in the lives of most of us we are at war. Over and over again we have tried to find a peaceful way out of the differences between ourselves and those who are now our enemies. But it has been in vain. We have been forced into a conflict. For we are called, with our allies, to meet the challenge of a principle which, if it were to prevail, would be fatal to any civilised order in the world.

It is the principle which permits a State, in the selfish pursuit of power, to disregard its treaties and its solemn pledges; which sanctions the use of force, or threat of force, against the sovereignty and independence of other States. Such a principle, stripped of all disguise, is surely the mere primitive doctrine that might is right; and if this principle were established thoughout the world, the freedom of our own country and of the whole British Commonwealth of Nations would be in danger. But far more than this—the peoples of the world would be kept in the bondage of fear, and all hopes of settled peace and of the security of justice and liberty among nations would be ended.

This is the ultimate issue which confronts us. For the sake of all that we ourselves hold dear, and of the world's order and peace, it is unthinkable that we should refuse to meet the challenge.

It is to this high purpose that I now call my people at home and my peoples across the seas, who will make our cause their own. I ask them to stand calm, firm, and united in this time of trial. The task will be hard. There may be dark days ahead, and war can no longer be confined to the battlefield. But we can only do the right as we see the right, and reverently commit our cause to God. If one and all we keep resolutely faithful to it, ready for whatever service or sacrifice it may demand, then, with God's help, we shall prevail.

May He bless and keep us all.

MOTHERS
Send them out
of London

Give them a chance of greater safety and health

3 Operation Pied Piper

The great evacuation of nearly one and a half million schoolchildren, mothers and babies from the danger zones of the United Kingdom was one of the most remarkable achievements of the first days of the war. Beginning before the sun rose on the morning of Friday 1 September this veritable army was transported in just under four days to new homes in the country thanks to 3000 buses (routed along main roads turned into single-direction carriageways), 4000 special trains, and close to 12,000 volunteer helpers.

That morning, as Hitler's forces stormed into Poland, so the children of the cities of England left their homes and caused what many people would later ruefully describe as an 'invasion' of a very different kind. For despite the warmly nostalgic picture that has for years been painted of this great evacuation, there was also undoubtedly conflict, unhappiness and even deep resentment on both sides.

For at least two years prior to what the Minister of Health, Mr Walter Elliot, would describe as 'an exodus bigger than that of Moses . . . the equivalent to the movement of ten armies', the Government had been concerned about the numbers of mothers and children living in the nation's cities who would probably be killed in the event of the air raids which would inevitably be targeted upon them. The answer, it seemed, would be to move these people into the private homes of those living in the 'safer' countryside. There would be no compulsion placed on the mothers and children to leave their homes if they did not wish to, but – if necessary – the Government would make the billeting of the evacuees compulsory. In return for taking in children, it was stated, each householder would receive eight shillings and sixpence per week per child.

The announcement that the evacuation was to begin was given out over the radio on the evening of the last night of August, allowing parents to make their obviously difficult decisions and pack what clothing they might require. Despite the widespread anxiety that existed about the terrors of bombing and poison gas, it still remains a fact that only about one-third of the mothers, babies and children who were expected to join this vast 'Operation Pied Piper' actually did so. A natural concern about being parted from their children – especially as war had not yet been actually declared – was doubtless one factor that influenced these parents;

another may well have been what can be seen only in hindsight as an unnecessary decision by the Government to keep the destinations to which the evacuees were being taken a secret.

There was, though, an atmosphere of optimism, even excitement, among the children and their mothers when they said goodbye to their homes on that Friday morning. A correspondent of *Time and Tide* magazine writing on 6 September had this to report on events in the capital: 'The evacuation from London will be long remembered by the young evacuees as a star turn in adventure and by the rest of us as a star turn in organization. I watched my nearest school start last Friday, neatly arranged by grown-ups wearing white LCC armlets into an immense excited crocodile, chattering like a thousand starlings and waved off with cheers by a crowd of mothers with babies, elder sisters and neighbours.

'On Sunday morning I saw some of those mothers and babies again, being shepherded by the efficient white armlets into an evacuation bus just as the sirens began. The Air-Raid Warden came whistling down the street, very worried about the situation, but the bus driver was firm about his instructions to get away as quick as he could and, his passengers being quite unruffled and the sky quite empty save for the balloon barrage majestically mounting like a herd of silver guinea-pigs, off he went with his load of babies. The conductor said it was one good thing anyway that someone had the idea of getting kids out of it.'

Howard Marshall, the writer and social historian, who also watched the evacuation from London at first hand in one of the main-line stations, observed some rather stronger emotions at work.

'It's no good saying that it was an easy thing to watch,' he wrote on 7 September. 'The moment came when wives and husbands had to part, for no relations could be allowed on the platform, and husbands would stretch across the barriers, holding for as long as possible to a child's hand. Those were moving moments. In them you could see summed up this sudden separation of families which the threat of war must mean, and which so many of us have to bear tonight. But even then at these sad barriers there were no scenes – just that extraordinary cheerful courage – and if relations were upset, as of course they were, they didn't show it until the mothers had gone, trudging down to the lifts, clutching their burdens, helping one another, patient and orderly.

'I went down in the lifts with them, and through those narrow underground passages where there might have been chaos – panic even – but not a bit of it. Even the tiniest children kept cheerful. I hardly heard a child cry once. And the steadily flowing detachments waited

One of the government posters urging the removal of children from the 'danger zones'.

Two official photographs released by the Censor to the press on 3 September in order to create the picture of a nation of children happily evacuated to the safety zones. The reality, however, was somewhat different.

EAST·KENT

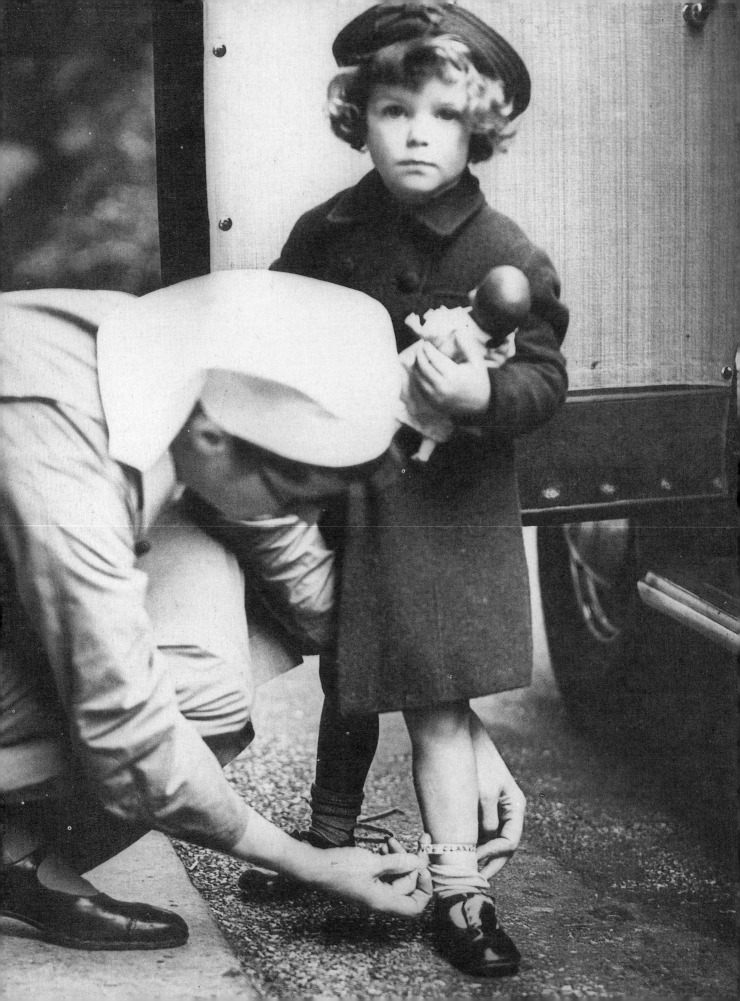

Uncertainty and even anxiety were often to be seen on the faces of many evacuated children. (Opposite) A matron checking a little girl's identification band, one of which was attached to each child's ankle before they left London for the country; and (above) a group of youngsters from the capital arriving at their billet in Eastbourne.

*Despite the upheaval of evacuation, moments of
humour did occur, inspiring cartoons like these two
typical examples by J. H. Dowd and Paul Sillince.*

"You're lucky to be able to have soap in your eye. In Germany the poor little boys can't have soap at all!"

for their lifts, filed in and out, followed their guides, and so smoothly and quietly into their trains. It was strange to watch this pilgrimage of women, and good to see how everyone helped – policemen carrying babies, and porters and LCC officials all lending a hand – a strange experience, as the whole evacuation has been. A people on the move – that's what it was – never in history has there been such a swift movement of population, and one may well wonder what the effects will be.'

Awaiting the arrival of this tide of evacuees at the other end of their trek were people such as the radio reporter John Hilton who reported what he saw on the Home Service a week later.

'What a time the children are having! Some have been homesick. Some are difficult. But the vast majority are having the time of their lives. Who will ever tell the full tale of their excitements and adventures? Who's ever going to tell one-tenth the tales of their doings and sayings?

'I like the answer of the child who was asked what part she'd come from. She said, "From England, Miss". And a dear friend of mine on a housing estate whose wife has taken two youngsters aged five from Hounslow tells me enough delightful things about them to fill half a book – their wonder when the potatoes were dug up in the patch. "What did you hide them for?" they said. "Was it for the war?" And the one of these two boys who got a letter from his father with a postal order for a shilling in it; and the other,

Evacuee. *"Wot's pushing it?"*

who seems not to have had a father, at once invented a super-splendid father who was going to send him in a day or two not just a shilling but half-a-crown. His father, he said, so far from driving a lorry with six wheels like the other boy's father, drove a lorry with twenty wheels, and he was sure to send the half-a-crown tomorrow. It didn't come; but by tomorrow it didn't matter, for he'd been sent on errands which had earned him sixpence and someone had just happened along and given him another sixpence. Well, who wants a father when things like *that* happen!

'The only trouble with these two little visitors is that they have voices against which a mere siren makes a poor show. If one of them mislays and calls out for his Snakes and Ladders the windows rattle and the dogs across the street begin to bark. My friend thinks their voices must be the result of having to make themselves heard above the roar of London's traffic. He and his wife have every confidence that in time they'll learn it isn't necessary to speak so loudly and they'll learn that between games there are better and safer places to sit than on the kerbstone with their feet in the gutter!'

John Hilton had clearly sensed that not every evacuee child was happy. Some had been billeted in understanding homes where the residents were prepared to make allowances for their obviously different lifestyles. Others, though, were not so lucky.

One such unhappy soul was a little urchin lad named Tom Bell from Liverpool who was to grow up to become one of the country's finest dramatic actors.

Then, he was just one of the eight children of a merchant seaman who lived in a tiny house and often slept three or four to a bed. Hard though those early days in Liverpool were – and Tom was used to being regularly beaten by his father ('people were like that – they just had kids for the sake of having them and then got rid of them,' he recalls today) – what happened to him in September 1939 has remained even more painfully etched on his memory.

'I was just six years old when my mother hung this label round my neck and sent me off to be an evacuee,' he says. 'They sent me to Morecambe, and in the very first place I stopped at, the son of the household looked me up and down and then deliberately spat in my face.

'After that I was shunted from one house to another. Sometimes I had to take cold baths while the rest of the family had hot ones. I also had to stand absolutely still and watch while one family ate their tea – I only got to eat mine when they had finished. It taught me to hide my feelings and grow a tough shell which I've never lost.'

But it was not only the evacuee children who encountered problems. The writer R. C. K. Ensor, living in a typical reception town in the Home Counties, noted the horror which some of the evacuee mothers and their infants had engendered in their new hosts.

'On the first day,' he wrote in *The Spectator* on 8 September, 'the incomers were mostly schoolchildren with teachers and escorts, and their numbers were well within the accommodation that had been arranged. The spirit of helpfulness shown all round was magnificent; the billeting officers, the housewives and the car owners all striving with inexhaustible patience and good temper to fit the pieces of the jigsaw puzzle together. The next day brought a much severer strain.

'Instead of schoolchildren and teachers, for which it was scheduled, the place suddenly had thrown at it from London a mass of mothers with younger children. Now the task of accommodating, say, two children or an adult is very different from that of accommodating a mother with children; and households ready for the one were quite unequal to facing the other. What made it worse was that many of the new arrivals were the lowest grade of slum women – slatternly malodorous tatterdemalions trailing children to match – whereas most of the houses in the reception area were those of prosperous artisans with neat, clean homes and habits of refinement. Why London suddenly forced such a problem on us was not explained; the conjecture was that a flood of last-hour applications from mothers had overwhelmed the despatching end. Few homes could even on paper take in the new-comers, and most of those that could were up in arms against doing so.

'A great deal of revision and re-adjustment was required. A house that had taken boys wanted to exchange with one nearby which had taken girls. Children from the same family or the same class were brought together. The London teachers, who had been round their children's billets, made many practical suggestions. Victims on whom slum mothers had been billeted, and who had already found their quarrelsomeness, acquisitiveness, and dirt utterly intolerable, insisted on and obtained release.'

The Spectator's postbag in the days that followed quickly showed that this was no isolated incident. A writer signing him- or her-self 'A Victim' wrote on 15 September congratulating the magazine on being 'the only paper which has broken the careful conspiracy of lies, organized on the Nazi model, to blanket the hardships inflicted on the victims in the "safe" areas'.

The writer continued: 'Apart from the disgraceful insistence of the billeting people in thrusting filthy women and children into the homes of decent, cleanly people, there is an economic hardship not yet mentioned. Many of the evacuated children arrived with no change of various undergarments. This means that the struggling country worker's wife must buy new socks and vests for the slum children or allow them to become even more malodorous than they are already.

'Then there is the case of the working wife who goes out to daily service to help with the rent money. She is now confronted with keeping two evacuees on 17 shillings a week, spending all her time on their cleaning, washing and cooking (subject to local busybodies' "inspection") and so losing her own job and wages. Again – aged people. I know of two retired folk: the husband 70, the wife 68. Both simple, childless, quiet people with no hobbies but their little spotless home and garden. Into this the billeting officer threatened to thrust three urchins. The couple, in dread of the prospect, said they would shut their cottage and go away. The official retort was that the cottage would be commandeered as soon as it was unoccupied. These cases can be multiplied endlessly.'

In the same letters column, 'A Northern Volunteer' – excusing his pseudonym because 'my address would disclose information which it is perhaps prudent to keep secret' – praised R. C. K. Ensor's article for 'the extreme moderation of its language, because it is

Women played a major part in the great evacuation, thanks to this poster campaign.

Schooling for the evacuated children continued wherever possible – this primary school for infants was in Harrogate.

obvious to all who have had any experience of reception that there has been a lamentable breakdown in the system in many directions, with lasting and unfortunate results for the evacuees and their hosts'.

He added: 'The evacuation scheme, like many Ministerial schemes, perfect on paper, took little or no account of the human element. It assumed, having directed the evacuation of so many thousand persons, and having directed their reception by so many thousand householders, that round and square pegs would automatically fall into round and square holes. It did not and could not work that way. When I read the Ministry of Health's unctuous and self-satisfied congratulations on the success of the scheme, I can only wish some official of that Ministry had been present here at our reception.'

The evident hostility which greeted the newcomers in a number of places was particularly felt by the evacuated mothers, and there is on record a letter from a young London mother to a friend back in the capital which evidence suggests is typical of a considerable number more that were written at this time. The original letter has been slightly adapted to make for easier reading.

'I am writing to let you know I have left Dunstable and am at my sister's,' the mother of two began. 'I couldn't stick it any longer – we were treated as bits of dirt by the locals. As if that wasn't bad enough going through what we did to get there. We started out at 11 o'clock and didn't get to Dunstable until 5 p.m. after five changes by train and bus and standing on the kerb in Luton for an hour and twenty minutes.

'We arrived at the skating rink and then were picked out – so you can guess what some poor devils were like who had four or five children: they were still there on the Sunday afternoon! Then eight families were put in an empty house and different people gave them bits of furniture. I admit some of them were a bit too much with their hair in curlers and overalls, but we were not all the same.

'I was lucky. I was in a very nice house and spotlessly clean. It was a Warden's post, but I felt in the way as they were so busy and if I'd stayed there I could only see my husband about every four weeks – but down here I can see him two or three times a week (I hope!)'

It is clear from these testimonies about what was nicknamed by some of its victims 'the slave market' that the evacuation scheme was badly flawed. But undoubtedly, too, a considerable number of the children and mothers – particularly those from the big city slum areas – benefited from their new lives in the fresh country air when they and their hosts took the trouble to come to terms with each other. Diligent country wives conducted a vigorous delousing campaign on

their guests, cured many of bed-wetting and then introduced them to cleaner ways and healthier diets.

By contrast, in certain more remote parts of the country, fewer children actually arrived than were expected, producing a very different reaction. Reporting one such incident in the House of Commons, Ellen Wilkinson said: 'I have heard the most charming stories from little Weardale villages on the moors where the whole population came out to welcome the children and the mothers, and there were women who went home weeping because they had not had a child allocated to them.'

And speaking during the same debate about what he saw as the core of the problem, Labour MP T. M. Sexton condemned those who were being deliberately obstructive. 'It seems to come from people living in moderately big houses and who, in times like jubilees and coronations are very much in the limelight, but now when they have been called upon to do a real job of patriotic work they have hardened their hearts and barred their doors to the evacuees from the poor areas.'

In hindsight, while it is possible to see that many dirty and undisciplined children were thrust upon households that had the utmost difficulty in coping with them, it is equally true that thousands of perfectly decent youngsters and mothers with babies were put into billets which fell far below the standards they were used to.

To HARASSED HOSTESS of Evacuated Children. Lady accustomed to management of her own staff and her father's large establishment offers her services; is willing to act as housekeeper and be a buffer between unexpected guests, servants and mistress. She might be able to bring her own head housemaid with her. Box D.656.

Advertisement from *The Times*, 6 September 1939

The inevitable result of all these unforeseen problems was that within a matter of a few days numbers of the city wives began to return home. Some had the money to travel by public transport; others hitched lifts or simply just walked. Some children, too, hankered after their parents, and scribbled desperate pleas to be collected by mothers or fathers, who would then arrive muttering darkly, 'Who's going to pay for this evacuation? Us mugs, I suppose. Money wasted, that's what it is. And it cost me a pound to bring my kid home!' According to the official figures, by 8 January 1940 almost 900,000 of the evacuated adults and children had gone home: though when the threat of invasion emerged in May 1940, the whole process began again, though much better conducted and more happily resolved on all counts.

The teachers who had accompanied their evacuated pupils in those early September days soon found that their job was now a full-time one – for not only had they to teach their children as best they could, but act as surrogate parents to those of their charges who were unhappy in their new surroundings. Yet, aided by parents and clergymen, the business of educating the future generation was able to continue, albeit under very trying circumstances.

One teacher evacuated to Brighton reported: 'The first week of evacuation was unbearable. The rumours of lousy, dirty, ill-behaved children bandied about

Brighton were exasperating. We knew that 90 per cent of the children were well behaved and happy. But the only stories regaled to me were the horrors of the wild London children. We check up in every case. Each teacher visited sixteen children, "her beat", twice a week for the first month for reports.'

One unusual suggestion for curbing bad behaviour was the imposition of an 8 p.m. curfew on all children! This was made at Chester Police Court on 5 September by Inspector Paul of the NSPCC who invited the magistrate to order all children indoors at that hour. Pointing out that he had no powers to make such an order, the magistrate urged Inspector Paul to communicate his 'admirable suggestion' to the Home Office, 'so that national action be taken'. Nothing further was, perhaps fortunately, heard of this draconian proposal!

However, for all the reports of unruly behaviour, it is a fact that apart from uncountable scratched arms and bruised knees there was only a single, sad fatality at this time. Six-year-old Michael Moscow of Stoke Newington, who was evacuated to a farm at Hallaton near Market Harborough in Leicestershire, was shot dead on 2 September by his elder brother while they were playing with a gun in some outhouses.

Undoubtedly one great calming influence amidst all these problems was the Queen, who undertook a busy schedule of touring the country to visit the evacuated families. So impressed was she by what she saw that she wrote a letter of thanks to the nation's new army of foster mothers.

'I wish to mark, by this personal message, my appreciation of the service you have rendered to your country,' she said. 'In the early days of the war you opened your doors to strangers who were in need of shelter, and offered to share your home with them.

'I know that to this unselfish task you have sacrificed much of your own comfort, and that it could not have been achieved without the loyal co-operation of all in your household. By your sympathy you have earned the gratitude of those to whom you have shown hospitality and by your readiness to serve you have helped the State in a work of great value.'

These warm words from the much-loved Queen healed many a grievance and eased many an antagonism, and with the passing of the days of that autumn, what were in effect two different peoples began to live together. The evacuation may not have been the success that had been envisaged (and the failure of the war to encroach on the country at that time was a significant factor), nor had it broken down the strong class feelings which existed, but it certainly began to ease them and was undoubtedly the first step towards the great revolution in social reform which was to produce the Welfare State in 1945.

Preparing for the German bombers – a London housewife sticking brown paper across her windows to prevent flying glass. Behind this hung the blackout curtains.

4 Life in the Unlit City

The lights went out all over the nation for the first time on the night of Friday 1 September, and the country began what for many people was to prove the most exasperating part of the early days of the war. For when the German raiders – for whom the lights had been switched off – failed to materialize, people found life every evening a series of continuing hazards and frustrations.

Today, it may seem hard to imagine what it must have been like to live in a world where overnight it became an offence against the law to allow *any* light to be visible in a building. But fortunately Tom Harrison, the mastermind of the Mass Observation Unit which collected data right through the war years, has provided us with a most evocative description, which he wrote in the autumn of 1939.

'The first impression of the first night of the blackout was psychological rather than physical,' he said. 'How weird! How rather exciting! How like the unseen forms of indigestion dreams! This groping through familiar streets now unfamiliar, all around you shadows which might turn out to be people or pillar-boxes, while sudden shapes of cars crawl up to you with eyes no more than cats'. This contradiction in our civilization, the unlit city, continues to bewilder for the first thirty seconds every time you go out of doors at night. On dark nights it is really a matter of groping one's way, with nerves as well as hands held out into the future of the next second.

'In the first weeks of war even small torches were not supposed to be used, though now plenty carry these, and we have the new dream situation where six or seven strangers walk in a formless crocodile behind the lady with the torch. But on moonlight nights, city dwellers have been forced to discover that not only do they live in a city, they also live under the heavens and patterns of the stars.

'Nothing, no amount of experience makes you really used to the black-out. And however little it may change your habits, the consciousness of it, waiting for you out there, behind the black material of the window, is a threat to any of the pre-war happy-go-lucky. Each evening expedition is now an event, maybe a dangerous adventure. For when the bright lights of a city are turned off, bright life is turned off, too.'

It was actually as early as July 1939 that the Government had distributed what was to be the first of several leaflets describing how all doors and windows could be made light-proof by the use of close-fitting blinds, old blankets or sheets of thick paper. 'In the event of war,' the leaflet had said, 'one of our great protections against the dangers of air attack after nightfall would be the "black-out".'

This simple reference in fact coined the term 'blackout', which in a short space of time was to become one of the most frequently used and enduring terms of the entire war. Curiously, one reader of *Notes and Queries* was so anxious about committing the expression to record that he wrote to that august journal of information in June 1940: 'In accordance with a recent suggestion in your pages, I start a list of new words which the war has produced. The "black-out" since September last, which has ordered us to shroud all sources of light at our windows at and during stated times, has been painfully familiar to householders, but the word may be forgotten in later years.'

Certainly, though, no one alive in those September

A government poster which offered some invaluable advice to the unwary during the blackout!

Issued by the Ministry of Health and the Department of Health for Scotland.

FIRST AID IN BRIEF

Read this carefully several times, then carry it in your pocket or bag

AFTER AN AIR ATTACK First Aid Parties will reach the wounded within a few minutes. Even such a short time counts. The man or woman on the spot can save lives by immediate and proper action.

Be prepared to see severe wounds. Be courageous and keep your head. Keep your mind on your duty to your injured fellow man.

Everyone in these days of danger should carry several clean handkerchiefs or small towels. These can be used as bandages, and their inner laundered surfaces are quite suitable for application to open wounds as a first dressing.

Unless a patient is in a highly dangerous place you should treat him where he lies. To lift or drag the wounded can do serious damage. Your general rule is that the moving and transport should be left to trained parties.

The first and most important duty of the civilian helper who first reaches a casualty is to stop bleeding.

When you cut a thumb you naturally grab it firmly with the fingers of your other hand. That application of pressure to a bleeding wound is the correct thing to do in all cases.

TO STOP BLEEDING

Press on the bleeding point with fingers or hands. As soon as possible apply a clean thick pad of folded handkerchief or towel. Use an inner surface of your handkerchiefs or towels. Keep up the pressure through this pad. Bandage the pad firmly in position over the wound. Be sure that the dressing is applied firmly enough to control the loss of blood. If there is still oozing of blood past or through the pad renew pressure over the whole dressing.

BLEEDING FROM ARM OR LEG

Press on the wound with fingers or hands. Apply a clean thick pad as soon as possible. Keep up pressure through the pad. Bandage the pad firmly over th[e]
fabric b[...]
at a po[...]
limb is [...]
the tig[...]
not to [...]
have to [...]
it to th[...]
hospital [...]

AIR RAID PRECAUTIONS
FIRE FIGHTING EQUIPMENT

TO REMOVE BOMB

REDHILL SAND CONTAINER
with
SCOOP AND HOE

In accordance with the
Home Office Specifications

TO PUT OUT
THE FIRES

'MINIMAX'
HAND FIRE
EXTINGUISHER

*A self-contained appliance
ready at all times for
immediate use*

Particulars of the above and other A.R.P. equipment upon request

MINIMAX LTD. (Box 173) **FELTHAM**
MIDDLESEX
('MINIMAX'—Registered Trade Mark)

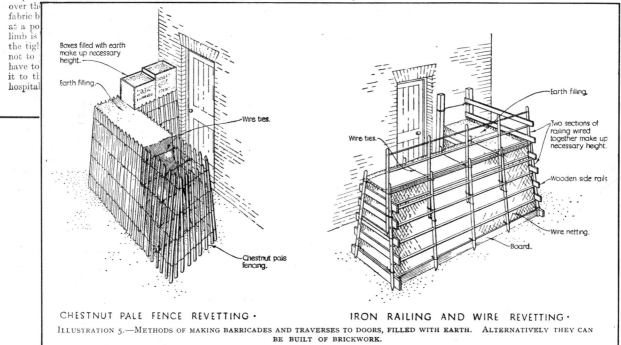

CHESTNUT PALE FENCE REVETTING ·   IRON RAILING AND WIRE REVETTING ·

ILLUSTRATION 5.—METHODS OF MAKING BARRICADES AND TRAVERSES TO DOORS, FILLED WITH EARTH. ALTERNATIVELY THEY CAN BE BUILT OF BRICKWORK.

Tips on how to survive in the blackout were offered in government leaflets, newspaper and magazine articles and even advertisements, as these typical examples from the beginning of the war show.

What to do when the syrens start

IF—
you're at home

IF an air raid comes, here are the complete details of what you should do.

First you must be sure that you can distinguish betwe[en] various signals given.

When enemy planes [are ap]proaching the air raid s[irens] give short blasts on a wavering note. Police and wardens will blow their w[histles].

Take cover at once. T[ake] gas mask with you wher[ever you] go. If there is gas you [are] warned by the sound [of] rattles; that means that [you] put on your gas mask a[t once].

When the raiders ha[ve gone] you will hear a continuo[us] note on the syrens. If [you] heard the hand rattles, [for] gas, wait until you hear [the] bell, which means that t[here is no] longer any gas danger.

Make sure that all the [members] of the household know [the mean]ing of these signals.

★

THE moment the alarm, g[oes] go to the your house or near it. [You] must know where this [is]. have an Anderson s[helter] see that it has plenty [on] top, because it is the e[arth that] gives protection agains[t] splinters—not the steel.

Make it face some [stout] wall or building, so t[hat a bomb] will not find its way in[side.] Have a piece of boar[d or corru]gated iron to stop f[lying splinters] entering the door.

★

IF you hav[e no] steel shelt[er or] room in yo[ur house seek] a refuge room. The[best ones] are on the ground [floor or] basement.

If you use the cell[ar, see that] there is another wa[y out, so that] you can't be caught i[f bombs block] the entrance.

Pasting strips of [paper cross]

cross over the windows is a good way to stop cracking from the blast of distant bombs.

★

BEFORE you leave your house, turn off the gas from the main. Do not turn off the electricity. You will want light and a radio set. Keep a few electric torches in the house.

Do not cut off the water, but keep some stored in the bath in case the mains are damaged. You may need the water for fire fighting.

Lay in some simple fire-fighting gear if you have not already done so. Buckets and a stirrup hand pump with thirty feet of hose are [all you need]

fence, Sir John Anderson, has emphasised that the worst danger in a raid is from flying splinters and debris.

Follow the signs leading to public shelters or trenches. If you are not near one seek shelter in the nearest substantial building. A deep doorway, a narrow passage between buildings, a stout archway, all will give protection.

If you're driving a car—

DO the same thing. Pull into the side so you will not impede ambulances and fire engines. Switch your engine off. Then go [to shelter.]

nearly always avoided by seeking shelter in any well-built premises.

Do's and Dont's

FIRST do not panic. This is most important. You only frighten other people unnecessarily. Run to your shelter but don't shout. Let the wardens do the shouting. It is their job to get people into shelters quickly and give them directions.

Obey every instruction the warden gives. He knows what he is doing. If there is no warden anywhere, don't dash frantically up and down the street. Seek shelter, [even if it is not so substantial as]

MAKE YOUR OWN BLACK-OUT FRAMES

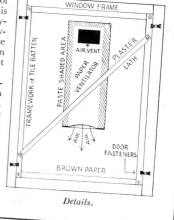

By TREVOR HOLLOWAY

DURING the first week of the black-out I wasted at least half an hour every evening fitting up an odd assortment of materials to screen the windows.

I resolved that such a state of affairs must be remedied, and now I can effectively screen six windows in as many minutes. This is how I set about it.

First of all I measured the windows and purchased sufficient timber to construct six light wooden frames. I used ¾-in. tile batten, costing ½d. per foot, and a number of plaster laths, at twelve for 6d. These laths were used for keeping the main frames square and rigid.

Screws were used for making the frames, as nails are apt to split the wood and the finished job is not nearly so rigid.

To these frames I pinned sheets of stout brown paper, purchased from my stationer. Each sheet measured 36 in. × 46 in., and cost 2d. If you buy several sheets there is generally a reduction in price.

Coarse brown packing paper can also be used. It is of denser texture; but very often contains a number of "pinholes". Ask to see each kind before making your purchase. The size and cost are about the same.

To keep the covered frames in position, use cupboard door fasteners, as shown in the diagram. They cost only 1½d. each. You will need four—one screwed to each corner of the window-frame. In two instances I had to mount the fasteners on small blocks of wood, as the covered frame was not quite flush with the window-frame.

To illustrate how easily the system works, I have

just blacked-out my own study window in less than one minute.

Although I have found the use of brown paper quite satisfactory, some of my neighbours have covered their frames with old pieces of floor-cloth and even odd sheets of wallpaper painted with black distemper. This last suggestion is not entirely satisfactory, as the paper is easily damaged.

Many people are rather dubious of using paper for black-out purposes, in case it should catch fire. This danger can be averted if the brown paper is painted with a strong solution of alum. This will render it fireproof.

One of the chief drawbacks of a black-out is the stuffiness of the room. I surmounted this problem by cutting a small aperture in the brown paper. Over this hole I pasted a long narrow strip of paper, as seen in the diagram. This ventilator was pasted on three edges only. The lower edge was left free, and when the window is left open a welcome draught of fresh air passes into the room, but no light is visible from outside.

In the case of small windows, it is possible to use plywood or straw-board, and for these materials a wooden framework is not essential.

The cheapest plywood is 2s. 6d. for a sheet measuring 5 ft. square; but the standard grade costs 5s. Strawboards (stiff brown cardboard) can be purchased in sheets measuring 25 in. × 30 in., and cost 4d. or 6d. each.

Details.

An Air-Raid Precaution Warden – ARP Warden for short – reporting 'All peaceful' in her area after a night patrol in September 1939.

days could imagine forgetting the term which dictated their every move once night had fallen. Yet, despite the determined efforts of officialdom to ensure that the country remained as 'blacked out' as was humanly possible, there were still some curious anomalies. For instance, lights could be seen on the railways, factories working night shifts glowed in the darkness, and many RAF pilots reported that the lights of cars on the roads beneath them could be seen 'like strings of diamonds' – despite the fact that they were supposed to be masked.

A frequently heard cry during the early days of the war was, 'Put that b— match out!' as nervous smokers lit up, forgetting the regulations. Indeed, one unfortunate man in Bridgend, Glamorgan was arrested and taken to court for striking a match on the night of 4 September – and not even the explanation that he had been looking for his false teeth saved him from being fined!

Yet, when air raids became a real possibility, it is true to say that the population responded with admirable speed to obscure every light. There were special problems, of course, for large office blocks, factories with skylights and churches with their Gothic windows – yet all these problems were solved, sometimes most ingeniously. Several major companies, for instance, painted the windows of their premises black and clamped them shut – despite the hothouse conditions this produced for their workers – while a number of enterprising clergymen simply switched their evening services to the afternoon! Many shopkeepers also augmented the blinds which they drew across their display windows by piling sandbags around the front of their premises. But what everyone was agreed upon was the unconscionable time that it took to black out any building, for even the owner of a modest semi-detached house might expect to be busy for as long as an hour each night ensuring that no chinks of light were visible from the street.

Such, in fact, was the demand created for the items needed for the blackout that the first great shortages of the war proved to be raw materials needed for it such as sateen cloth and brown paper, followed quickly by torch batteries which one wag later described as becoming 'more valuable than letters from the front!' Advertisers, on the other hand, were quick to spot the advantages presented by the blackout.

Optrex, for instance, promoted their preparation for easing tired eyes with the slogan 'Black out causes eye strain!'; while Osram, the electric light manufacturers, in claiming their bulbs were brighter than others, urged customers to 'Light up – and smile'. 'Dim lights and low spirits never won anything,' said an Osram advertisement, 'certainly not the "war against boredom" on the home front that we are counselled to wage. So light

up your home and you will light up the hearts of all about you. You do not have to cut down your electricity – and your black-out precautions should be a little more permanent anyway. Also good light will ease your eyes and your temper, too, by making your rooms the cheerful places that they used to be!'

The actual responsibility for ensuring that no lights were visible from buildings fell on to the police force and the Air-Raid Wardens – though it was the men in blue who were the only ones who could specifically *order* a light to be diminished or put out.

The Air-Raid Precaution Wardens – or ARP Wardens as they were usually called – had first been mooted in 1937 following the realization by the Government of the danger of air raids in any war, and they were, in effect, an army of volunteers drawn from all sections of the population – with perhaps the larger percentage coming from the upper and middle classes. In almost all areas of the country, there were virtually twice as many men as women serving as wardens. Initially the ARP personnel were unpaid volunteers, but on the outbreak of war they all became salaried staff.

Although the signs are clear enough that the vast majority of these wardens – whose job it was to patrol a specified area watching for any untoward light, checking on the safety of the residents and being alert for the tell-tale smells of poison gas (which could resemble the odour of musty hay, geraniums or peardrops) – were dedicated, kindly but firm people, there were others who abused their powers and earned the dislike of everyone with whom they came into contact.

Certainly the cause of even the best of these men and women was not helped by the lack of enemy action in the first few months of the war. One fifty-year-old warden probably spoke for a considerable number of his colleagues when he remarked just before Christmas 1939: 'I've a good mind to chuck it all up. If there had been an air raid we would all be public heroes. As it is, we're called wasters and slackers.'

C. D. Newman, an Air-Raid Warden in Hertfordshire from the onset of the war, has vividly recalled, in a diary entry he made for the first week of October, what life was like for men and women such as him in these early days of the 'phoney war'.

'We have been waiting since midnight for the raiders' he noted. 'Every night we have been waiting since midnight. Already we have been at it for three hours and hardly a sound has disturbed our waiting. Here in the brilliantly-lit interior of the ARP Control Centre we sit and watch the blackboard with its listing of ambulances, fire engines, stretcher-parties, decontamination squads.

'Now and then someone opens a fitful conversation – something about being a funny war with leaflets being

Fifty years of the Anderson shelter! (Above) A London mother, Mrs Ethel Markworth, and her children in their Anderson shelter following an air-raid warning; and (below) the author's daughter Gemma, emerging from the Haining family shelter which still exists today – as a brewing cellar!

EVERYMAN'S SHELTER
GARDEN TRENCH
SIMPLEST AND CHEAPEST

dropped instead of bombs. The conversation dies away. Someone else thinks it would be an idea to have a cup of tea. We have it. You can hear the click of knitting needles from the women in the next room. From the two sleeping figures on their camp beds come queer animal noises. A car has just purred through the sleeping village outside. It's peace more tranquil than peace.

WHISTLE THAT CAUSED ALARM

A man who blew a whistle for his dog in Sherwood Street, Nottingham on Wednesday night (September 6) caused many people to run out of their homes thinking there was an air raid. This statement was made by a police sergeant yesterday at Nottingham Police Court where the man, Edward Gavagan, an ice cream salesman, was fined five shillings on a charge of being drunk and disorderly.

From the *Daily Mail*, 8 September 1939

'Suddenly the place is split with the ring of a phone bell. Everyone wakes up into instant action. Gasmasks are at the ready. Have they come at last? A messenger rushes in. Hastily scanning those vital words, the Controller moves quickly to the blackboard. He seizes a pin and moves it one space to the left, and the whole nerve centre knows that number three stretcher-party in area four has gone off to bed!'

There was already in place all over the country at the start of the war an air-raid warning system consisting of sirens which gave out a penetrating wail, quite unforgettable to anyone who heard them. The first use of these sirens actually occurred only a few minutes after the Prime Minister had finished his speech declaring war – at 11.28 a.m. to be precise. The ominous wail carried throughout Greater London, the Home Counties and East Anglia. There was no panic in the streets, as one or two commentators had actually feared, and in fact, in most places, men, women and children filed in orderly fashion into either their own air-raid shelters or those provided for their communities. When, half an hour later, the all-clear was sounded, there was almost a feeling of anti-climax among those who had half expected to emerge and find scenes of devastation all around them. Instead, the sunny and warm Sunday was continuing just as they had left it.

There were actually quite a number of people who

claimed that the sound of the siren was more terrifying than the thought of an air raid itself! For several days the letter columns of the daily newspapers contained suggestions for alternative sounds. Perhaps the most imaginative idea came from a *Daily Express* reader who suggested that the warning should be given by playing the opening bars of 'Colonel Bogey' and the all-clear sounded to the strains of 'Who's Afraid of the Big Bad Wolf'!

For Londoners, the best form of protection from any aerial raiders already lay beneath their feet: the Underground system. In the days prior to the declaration of war, work had been carried out to install floodgates in case the walls were breached by bombing and the entire system was flooded. As it was, millions of grateful citizens descended to the stations each night, and from their packed but happy communities called on Hitler to do his worst!

As far as the rest of the nation was concerned, families everywhere had cause to be grateful to the foresight of Sir John Anderson, the Home Secretary, who, by the beginning of the war, had distributed some one million of the domestic air-raid shelters named after him. These corrugated-iron structures reinforced with cement and piled over with soil offered protection for close on six million souls. And while it is probably true that quite a number still awaited erection on the day war was declared, with the threat of air raids now passing from being just talk to an imminent possibility, they sprang up with increasing speed: an estimated 2,300,000 capable of protecting four times that number of people were in place just one year later when the German air raids began in earnest. (In all, a total of six million of the shelters were handed out during the war, costing £7 each plus any labour charges – though any worker earning less than £250 per year qualified for an Anderson free of charge.)

Today, many thousands of these shelters still remain in the back gardens of suburban homes throughout the country, serving as storage rooms or – in the case of my own family – a cellar for my father's home-made wine and beer! And though they had their detractors, the Andersons were undoubtedly a great source of comfort when the sirens wailed and the drone of bombers was actually heard overhead.

In 1941, following a growing reluctance among many people to leave their homes to go into their shelters, the new Home Secretary, Herbert Morrison, had an indoor version devised rather like a large steel table which, ideally, could be installed under the stairs. Over a million of these 'Morrisons' were to be built, each one providing shelter for an average family of two adults and two children. Indeed, my own most enduring memory of the end of the war is of being rushed from the garden by my mother into such a shelter as one of the German V1 flying bombs, nicknamed 'Doodle-bugs', whined overhead. Mind you, I recall not being too pleased at the time because I would much rather have stayed where I was to see where the bomb fell!

One further significant event occurred in the first week of September which relates to the defence of the country. Percy Harris, the MP whose letter to *The Times* of 14 August 1914 had led to the formation of the Volunteer Training Corps in the First World War, wrote once again to the paper on 5 September urging the mustering of another similar force of amateur soldiers prepared to defend their country in the event of invasion. 'I believe,' he said, 'there are a great number of men over military age and men who are prevented because they are scheduled in reserve occupations who would like to train in the use of a rifle as well as to do part-time service.'

Here was the first suggestion for the band of men who were to be constituted in May 1940 as the Home Guard – that redoubtable force still as much a part of the folk memories of the war as the blackout, gas masks and even the Anderson shelters! And though their inauguration on 14 May falls outside the scope of this book, I have been fortunate in securing a few examples of their Standing Orders, which are reproduced over-leaf as a fascinating reminder of just how the real 'Dad's Army' went to war.

Have YOU Heard The Phantom Siren ?

◆

MYSTERY OF EERIE ALARMS

IS THIS what we have to run to earth if we are to capture the "phantom" siren player—a cyclist with a "portable"?

Inhabitants of St. Michael's Ward and the surrounding district, writes an "Independent" representative, are now becoming accustomed to the playful toot-ings of the phantom siren. But . . . !

For the last few weeks, at any hour at which it would seem the capricious operator desires amusement, the siren emits its wail, piping a curdling tune of portentous alarm.

An Air Raid Imminent?

When this mysterious practical joker—if he or she IS a practical joker—first began his musical practices in straight style, many residents stirred in their beds, awakened in the spine-tingling belief that an air raid was imminent, hurriedly donned clothes and assembled downstairs, anxiously awaiting the phantom's specially-devised "all clear" which follows, usually, five minutes later.

But now the siren has forsaken its erst-while measured notes and is attempting the rhythm of a "Tiger Rag" by a reiteration of brief toots.

This more frivolous style has failed to bestir the residents who, with a soft curse for the mysterious being who disturbs their rest, merely turn over, snuggle down, and again seek the ignorant bliss of sound sleep.

But, having given a few practice toots during the week-end, our modern Pan-piper

decided to settle down, early on Monday morning, to a really solid test, and

at about 6.15 or 6.20, for upwards of ten seconds, an "official" air raid warbling note wavered ominously on the still dawn air.

A week earlier the sound would have roused the district to air raid action.

But not so on Monday morning! Male residents cursed the siren roundly, reassured anxious wives, and were asleep again almost before the "all clear" sounded.

But, we repeat, where is this siren.

If He Is Captured!

I decided, writes an "Independent" representative, that I'd track the thing and its owner to its lair if it took me "a month of Sundays."

And then I'd know, too, what to do with the siren and its operator!

Unlike the hero of a thousand thrillers, shockers and detective preambles who, declines to call in the police until he has beaten up the villain, I sought the assistance of the police first.

But the police knew nothing of the phantom. In fact, they had not even had the privilege of listening to his nocturnal musical interludes. They assured me that it could not have been an official siren.

More than that they did not know, but

(continued on page 15)

Another very curious air-raid warning story from the **Northampton Independent** *of 13 October 1939.*

Subject:-   Calling out the Home Guard.

   C.R.N.C.2/30013/C(H.O.) dated 2 Oct 40 and 25 Oct 40 are cancelled and the
following is substituted:-

1. Role before an emergency.

    (a) Cases in which the Home Guard have been called out as a precautionary
        measure in an anticipated emergency show that the proper function of
        this Force has not always been fully understood.

    (b) The Home Guard consists of citizens who are dependent on their
        work for their daily bread and on whom the country is dependent
        for maintaining its industrial and agricultural output. The
        organisation aims at providing such citizens with the arms
        and training necessary to enable them to assist the armed forces
        in the defence of the country without interfering with their
        means of livelihood or their capacity for production. It is
        essentially a force of unpaid volunteers.

    (c) It follows, therefore, that the Home Guard must not be employed
        during periods when they should be occupied with their normal
        work, and hours of duty and training must be arranged accordingly
        unless and until an emergency actually arises.

2. When and how the Home Guard is called out.

    (a) If parachutes or other air-borne troops are actually seen landing
        by a Home Guard or military observer he will cause the church bells to
        be rung without delay. On this summons the local Home Guard will turn
        out. This signal is NOT to be repeated in any other locality in which
        parachute or other air-borne troops have not actually been seen landing.

    (b) To guard crashed aeroplanes until a military guard can be summoned.
        In this case the local Home Guard will be called out by the military
        or Home Guard Commander in the locality concerned. The method of calling
        the Home Guard will be by telephone, bicycle orderly, runner etc., but
        church bells will not be rung.

    (c) The message "STAND TO" will be sent to Corps and Areas by these
        Headquarters. This message will be repeated by Corps, through
        military channels, to all Home Guard units which have been ordered
        to turn out on "STAND TO".
            In order to avoid interference with their civilian occupations
        so far as possible all ranks of the Home Guard who turn out on
        "STAND TO" will only be required to man their posts for the period
        from $\frac{1}{2}$ hour before dawn until 2 hours after dawn each day until
        the threat has passed or "ACTION STATIONS" has been ordered.
            The method of turning out these units will be by telephone,
        bicycle orderly, runner etc.
            The message "STAND TO" will be repeated by Areas, and by County
        Divisions when they have assumed command, through Home Guard channels, to all
        units of the Home Guard which have not been detailed to turn out. The object
        of this is to enable the Home Guard Commanders concerned to make any
        necessary preparations to ensure that they can turn out their volunteers
        in the shortest possible time, if required to do so subsequently.

(d) When invasion actually occurs or if it is desired to increase the state of readiness, the order "ACTION STATIONS" will be sent to Corps and Areas by these Headquarters.
On receipt of this message all Home Guards who have not already been ordered out, will turn out and man their posts, including road blocks to 100%.
(Note:- 100% must be taken to mean 100% of the available men and not necessarily 100% of the total strength.)
The method of communicating the order to Home Guards will be by bicycle orderly, telephone, runner, etc.
The responsibility for communicating the order to each Home Guard unit will rest with the Military Commander in operational command of that unit.

(e) In the event of invasion coming as a surprise, whether the order "STAND TO" has been sent out or not, any Military Commander may order "ACTION STATIONS" to units of the Home Guard under his operational control.
The method of turning out the Home Guard will be as defined in para. 2 (d) above.

3. <u>Loss of wages.</u>

Instructions will shortly be issued in regard to compensation for loss of wages as a result of being called out for operational duties.

4. <u>Arrangements for ringing the bells.</u>

Arrangements for ringing the church bell must be fully organised in all cases. Military and Home Guard Commanders will ensure:-

(a) That someone is available at all times who is capable of ringing the church bell. In cases where no such person is now available arrangements must immediately be made for suitable persons to be instructed.

(b) That all concerned know where the persons referred to in 4 (a) above are to be found by day or night.

(c) That the bell in question is capable of being rung.

(d) That access to the church and belfry is available at all times.

In any cases where the arrangements are not complete and satisfactory the necessary action will be taken forthwith in conjunction with the incumbent of the parish.

Sgd .... Major
for Brigadier, General Staff,
NORTHERN COMMAND.

York
13 Mar 41.

COPY.

SECRET.

G.H.F. 1 5 59/G.

NOTES ON GERMAN PARACHUTISTS.

7. Troops must be careful not to shoot our own R.A.F. personnel who may be saving themselves by parachute from a damaged aircraft. As a guide it may be assumed that if more than six parachutes drop at once they will be enemy. If fewer than six are seen coming down, until it is certain that they are enemy, they should not be shot at.

    When parachutists are airmen in distress, either British or German, their aircraft will probably be seen or heard to crash in the neighbourhood at the same time.

8. The Air Ministry has issued the following instructions to R.A.F. personnel forced to land by parachute:-

    (a) When persons approach to apprehend them they should stand still holding both hands above their heads with fingers extended and announce their identity loudly. They should make no movement until their identity is established.

    (b) If ordered to produce proof of identity they should say where this can be found on them but should not lower their hands in case their action arouses suspicion that they are reaching for a weapon.

    (c) If injured they should lie flat and stay still.

                          (Signed) A.I. CD. GD. LL.,
                          For Lt.Gen.,
                          C.S.

Home Forces
G.O. G.P.O. London

13th June 1940

Y.A. 7517/25

COPY.

Subject:- Traffic Control - Road Blocks.

C.R.N.C. 2/22041/G(O) of 18.8.40 is reproduced below for information and necessary action.

A case occurred recently in which an ambulance taking a sick man to hospital was delayed for an unnecessarily long time at a road barrier whilst the sentry examined identity papers and pay books of the driver and orderlies who were in the ambulance. The patient subsequently died.

Steps would be taken to ensure that ambulances are enabled to pass sentry posts with the minimum delay consistent with security requirements.

                          (Sgd) A.K. KAY, Brigadier,
                          General Staff,
                          Northern Command.

York
18. Aug. 40

The original 'Dad's Army' – volunteers for the Home Guard learning the art of bayonet warfare. Here a bus conductor tries his hand while other new recruits look on.

5 An Army in Gas Masks

Arguably the greatest fear of all among the people of Britain when war was declared was the fear of being gassed. Although Parliament, the scientists and the military were divided in their opinions as to whether it was feasible – or even likely – that the Germans would bombard the country with poison gas, the Government was not prepared to take the risk, and by the time Chamberlain made his crucial decision, millions of the strange-looking masks officially described as 'civilian-type respirators' had been distributed to almost every man, woman and child in the nation.

Former London Home Guard, James Holmes of Battersea, remembers this aspect of the war very clearly. 'That Monday morning, everywhere you went people were carrying their masks. It was almost like an army with those brown cardboard boxes over their arms. The Government had certainly prepared for a gas attack very well – but perhaps because they had done it so well they made everyone more frightened it would actually happen. Of course, people weren't afraid for very long, and then the problem became all the masks that were mislaid or deliberately lost!'

The Government had coordinated its despatch of the masks during the previous months with a poster campaign which declared dramatically, 'Hitler will give no warning – So always carry your gas mask.' From factory worker to farm labourer, and from housewife to schoolchild, the Government ensured that Britons were far better prepared for any such attack than their counterparts in Germany – where, curiously, such equipment was issued only in the most desultory fashion throughout the war.

In Britain, memories of these masks vary from the comical to the nightmarish. They attracted a large number of nicknames from 'nose-bag' to 'dickey-bird', the favourite expression with children apparently being a 'Hitler'. They frustrated busy men who inadvertently forgot them on the way to work and were sent home to fetch them by zealous employers. And they drove a good many fashion-conscious women to despair trying to find a container for them which did not clash with their outfits!

In hindsight, it seems evident that for the first few weeks of the war gas masks were treated seriously by much of the population, but with the passage of time and the dwindling of fears about attacks of mustard gas or the even deadlier Lewisite gas, they soon became a novelty and finally an exasperation. On Monday 4 September, however, workers, housewives and children everywhere still had the words of one of the radio announcers from the previous afternoon ringing in their ears. This solemn individual had come on the air not long after the Prime Minister's broadcast to demand 'Have you all got your masks?' After a suitable

Hitler will send no warning –
so always carry your gas mask

ISSUED BY THE MINISTRY OF HOME SECURITY

Warnings of the danger of gas attacks had been posted everywhere throughout the nation by the time war broke out. Just some of the various government posters emphasizing the danger – and how to survive when the poison dropped.

pause, he had continued: 'If not, see your warden. If you do not know who he is, get in touch with the local council. Anyway, get a mask. When you get it, make sure it fits. Shorten or lengthen the straps and secure them with the safety pins and then put the mask where you can lay your hand on it. To sum up: find your gas masks, fit them, and then make sure you do not lose them!'

In actual fact, there were three types of masks. The most common was the civilian's mask with its small can-shaped filter and single plastic eye panel. The two others were both for use by civil defence workers. The 'civilian duty' type also had the can-shaped filter, but separate eye-pieces and a rubber ear-piece to enable the wearer to use the telephone. For those people who were likely actually to have to deal with gas canisters there were the heavy-duty masks with thick goggles and a rubber tube running to a supply of oxygen carried on the person.

Although it took only a matter of moments to put on the mask and adjust it, there were undoubtedly many people who experienced a sense of claustrophobia when wearing them. Because of their tight fit, the masks often steamed over after a few minutes of being worn – but it was soon discovered that a little soap applied to the inside of the eye piece prevented this.

HOW TO PUT ON YOUR GAS MASK

Always keep your gas mask with you – day and night. Learn to put it on quickly. Practise wearing it.

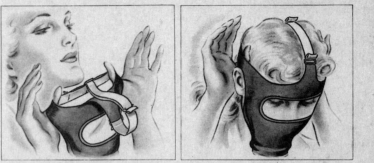

1. Hold your breath. 2. Hold mask in front of face, with thumbs inside straps.
3. Thrust chin well forward into mask, pull straps over head as far as they will go.
4. Run finger round face-piece taking care head-straps are not twisted.

IF THE GAS RATTLES SOUND

1. Hold your breath. Put on mask wherever you are. Close window.

2. If out of doors, take off hat, put on your mask. Turn up collar.

3. Put on gloves or keep hands in pockets. Take cover in nearest building.

IF YOU GET GASSED

BY VAPOUR GAS Keep your gas mask on even if you feel discomfort
If discomfort continues go to First Aid Post

BY LIQUID or BLISTER GAS

1	2	3	4
Dab, but *don't rub* the splash with handkerchief. Then destroy handkerchief.	Rub No. 2 Ointment well into place. *(Buy a 6d. jar now from any chemist).* In emergency chemists supply Bleach Cream free.	If you can't get Ointment or Cream within 5 minutes wash place with soap and warm water	Take off at once any garment splashed with gas.

PRINTED FOR H.M. STATIONERY OFFICE BY FOSH & CROSS LTD., LONDON   (51/504)

*A group of infants wearing their 'Mickey Mouse'
masks during a gas drill.*

Many small children were naturally suspicious, even frightened, of the masks, while others took to them with malicious delight, leaping out and terrifying younger brothers and sisters or friends. For toddlers, the authorities issued a rather less frightening mask which had large ears, was painted in red and blue, and was soon nicknamed the 'Mickey Mouse'.

For babies too young for this mask (that is, under the age of two) a special 'gas helmet' had been devised which was not unlike a miniature iron lung. Once inside this, the child was fed a supply of oxygen by means of a small pair of bellows which the mother operated. Despite specially run instruction courses, few parents were altogether happy with this appliance, and probably even fewer babies – if the many stories of infants being plucked from them red-faced and screaming at the end of demonstrations are to be believed!

Although there was no compulsion under law to carry a gas mask, there was a widespread rumour in

*A mother demonstrating the use of the special 'gas
helmet' devised for babies.*

"Mrs. Jones has got a new gas-mask carrier, dear."

Like so many other elements of the war, gas masks
were an inspiration to the British sense of humour, as
this Punch cartoon of 20 December reveals.

September 1939 that people *could* be fined for not having one about their person. The police were said to be empowered to stop anyone seen without their mask and fine them a sum which varied from five shillings (for a first offence) to five pounds for a persistent offender. One particular story from Essex insisted that a man had been fined fifteen shillings at Romford Police Court on Tuesday 5 September for going without his gas mask; and this story would not go away despite repeated denials from the clerk to the magistrates.

Even if there was no law about carrying a mask, many cinemas, theatres and other places of public entertainment would not allow patrons in unless they were carrying one. And many offices, shops and factories not only did their best to make sure their workers were always prepared should there be a gas raid, but some even held regular refresher courses during working hours to ensure they could don these appliances speedily and effectively. In the first week of September, reliable estimates put the number of civic-minded citizens who carried their gas masks as high as 70 per cent; but before the month was out this figure had dropped to below the half-way mark because of the growing conviction that a gas attack was unlikely.

The humour that the mask had already inspired was no doubt a strong contributing factor in this attitude. The Mass Observation Unit reported two typical comments from the streets of London on the third day of the war.

'Where's your bloody tin hat?' one man was heard to chide another carrying his mask over his shoulder. 'If you had bloody gumboots and decontamination outfit you'd come in wearing them, too!'

And in another incident, a woman was heard to ask a man where his mask was.

'I'm not carrying it,' he said. 'I'm not afraid.'

'Neither am I,' said the woman. 'I'm not carrying mine either.'

To which a woman on the opposite side of the street chimed in, 'Neither am I – *mine's* in a drawer at home!'

The Times found itself unintentionally drawn into an amusing situation following the publication in its usually staid letter column of a letter from a Mrs Peggy Pollard of St Mawes in Cornwall, in which she touched on the problems that men with beards were experiencing with their gas masks. Her original letter offering an ingenious solution, plus its humorous sequel, are both reprinted on these pages.

The newspaper cartoonists and magazine columnists were quick to make full use of the funny side of this developing situation. A columnist in the 20 September issue of *Punch*, for example, writing with his tongue firmly in his cheek, said: 'I saw a new gas-mask case in Oxford Street today, made of crushed moire silk with a soupçon of beige catafalque, embroidered with a portrait of Ribbentrop and a quotation from *The Merchant of Venice*. At eighteen guineas, including the real cowhide strap, it should be a popular model.'

If, initially, the gas mask had been seen as the life support against the terrors of gas attack, within a few weeks of the war becoming a reality, it was clearly regarded as rather more a symbol of amusement. None the less, even in that it had served a valuable purpose in making the people of Britain alert to the potential dangers of war.

GAS MASKS AND BEARDS
From: Peggy Pollard, The Ropewalk, St Mawes, Cornwall.

'Reading with concern of the men who have cut off their beards in order to put on their gas masks, may I put forward a suggestion for the comfort of bearded men who do not wish to lose this desirable ornament? Four curling-pins may be bought at the stores and the beard tightly rolled up in these and tucked under the chin. The gas mask is then drawn over the face, beard and all, and is perfectly airtight. This discovery has been the means of preserving my husband's magnificent beard, and I submit it to you in the hope that it may save others.'

* * *

'My letter to you about gas masks and beards has had vast repercussions. A French lady, enclosing a cutting from *L'Oeuvre* headed "L'Idée de Peggy", writes to ask if I really exist; the story has been broadcast from Stuttgart to show the utter demoralisation of Englishwomen in the face of "ces terribles avions allemands". A prominent weekly suggests that I do not in fact exist and that the Greatest of Newspapers has been hoaxed. This is the way in which cosmic nature-myths start, and in a thousand years or so the anthropologists of Oxford and Cambridge will have proved me to be an embodiment of the winter solstice, the beard a crop of mistletoe, and the gas mask an eclipse of the moon.'

From *The Times*, 28 September and 20 October 1939

6 On the Home Front

'Now that one of the greatest of all calamities has befallen us we must, in order to face it in the best possible manner, review our ways of life, must decide what things are essential and what can be discarded.' So the prestigious weekly magazine *The Lady* addressed its millions of readers in its first issue in wartime Britain. For the women of the nation, whatever their background and wherever they lived, the day that war broke out was to change their lives profoundly – though not immediately, for those two elements so associated with wartime, shortages and rationing, were still things of the future.

The Lady, though, was anxious that even in these first dark days, no woman should be allowed to forget that one of her prime duties was to remain *feminine*. She must, the magazine insisted, look to her wardrobe. 'Economies will be demanded, but in planning our outfits with our mind on the main qualities of comfort and durability we must not let ourselves forget their beauty. "I can't tell you what it meant to me to see you looking so young and pretty," a young soldier returning to France in 1916 after his four days' leave wrote to his mother, and his words are worth remembering now, when women will have to guard against setting an atmosphere of depression and gloom. We must endeavour to look well, however sad may be our hearts and however hard and long our working hours.'

Another leading women's journal, *Housewife* magazine, also urged its readers not to forget their looks. 'Some of us will be anxious, others lonely and tired. But isn't that just one more reason why you and I should include our faces in the scheme of decoration and cheer up ourselves and others? Isn't it worth that extra five minutes in the morning to be a cheerful sight? We must all put our best face forward!'

There can be no doubt, looking back over the gulf of fifty years, that the mothers, wives and girlfriends of Britain played as vital a role in the winning of the war against Germany as the sons, husbands and lovers who went off to fight it. Whether working in the factories or on the land, helping in voluntary organizations such as the Red Cross or WVS, or in the forces themselves, the women of Britain were a major element in achieving what would be a famous victory. Perhaps nowhere else, though, did they triumph quite so completely as in their own homes where they raised the children, provided the food, and maintained an unshakable resolve through everything that fate and Hitler could direct at them. And through all this, they managed to remain feminine with their prowess in terms of fashion, food and socializing intact – albeit that each and every one of these was now severely restricted!

In the realms of fashion the first trend was naturally for more women than ever before to be seen in uniform, while in civilian life skirts and hats (previously considered essential for every well-dressed woman) made way for headscarves and suits and overcoats modelled on military lines with padded shoulders and fake epaulettes. One problem that every woman faced was how to make her gas-mask container a little less obtrusive when carried on her arm, now that she must have it with her at all times. The variety and decorativeness of the containers which were swiftly launched on to the market were quite amazing, as the photographs from the *Illustrated London News* reproduced on page 73 clearly demonstrate!

One ingenious London fashion house, H. J. Nicoll of Regent Street, spotting another opportunity, launched what they called 'a specially designed gas protection costume in oiled silk'. This consisted of a trouser suit with mittens and a hood top which, it was claimed, could be slipped over the wearer's ordinary clothes in just 35 seconds. Nicoll's said that a woman dressed in the suit could cover a distance of at least two hundred yards through mustard gas and remain unharmed. Selling at forty shillings each, the gas protection costume was available in several 'gay pastel colours'. (Later in the war, siren suits complete with trousers were to become enormously popular and for the first time in history women were able actually to wear trousers in public without being laughed at!)

More than the threat of poison gas, though, it was underwear which presented a challenge immediately after Mr Chamberlain's declaration; for within days, shops were reporting a vastly increased demand for knicker elastic and stockings! As the women's page editor of the *Daily Telegraph* put it, 'Today tempting gear and alluring fabrics lie neglected in the shops, but the stocking counters are continually busy and a woman's only act of personal forethought in these days of preparation has been to replenish her stocking drawer. There is wisdom in this, for the old coats and dresses can be mended and brushed and dyed, or even become a little shabby before their wearer is depressed by their age or condition, but there is no way of dodging up silk stockings. It is not only their future scarcity and price that are feared, but the difficulty of keeping up appearances without them. The queer spectacle of clusters of stocking buyers in otherwise almost deserted shops is one of the things we shall remember and tell our grandchildren, perhaps, about the beginning of this war!'

The war made trousers fashionable for women – though the first girls to wear boiler suits in the street caused some surprise among their neighbours!

A warm wool dinner dress brings comfort and grace to your winter evenings. This model, in soft wool crêpe, has a draped bodice held by knots of satin. Price £5 19s. 6d. from the tea gown department of MARSHALL & SNELGROVE

WAR-TIME WARDROBE

YOU can't face a war without good clothes—and by good we mean warm, comfortable, well-fitting and fairly conservative clothes, and having a spark of gaiety about them, to cheer you and all those who see you. Banish all-black (though black with plenty of white accents is perky enough for anything), and take to the rich dark greens, fir and reseda, the big gamut of reds from rose to terracotta, the pinky browns and rich Chinese enamel combinations in tweed, which make gay the collections the shops are showing for autumn. Do your shopping early, for prices, particularly of wool and leather, will rise when the present stocks have run out; and buy wisely but boldly, remembering that you are not only giving yourself the best possible tonic, but helping the vital economy of the country.

Certain garments you are bound to want, and you should get them into your wardrobe if you don't own them already. You must have :—

A warm wool suit. War-time permits you to wear tweeds anywhere, but have them smooth and sleekly tailored if your life is mainly in town. Studd & Millington, in Chancery Lane, make superb tweed suits for round about seven guineas.

Left: Easy-to-get-into wool dress, which wraps round and ties at one side; two gilt leaf clips hold the neckline; price 98s. 6d.
DEBENHAM & FREEBODY

Right: Jumper suit in black and white bouclé jersey. The jumper has a black trellis fastening. 79s. 6d.
LONDON ASSOCIATION FOR THE BLIND

How to WIN YOUR WAR against wrinkles and tired skin

WOMEN war workers—you who are doing your duty to the nation—don't neglect your duty to yourself—to your sweethearts and husbands. It's a duty to take care of your skin—to look *young*. Out in all weathers—cold, wind and rain —more than ever to-day you need this Skin Specialist's advice to keep your skin soft, fresh, unlined and young.

A new precious extract of skin cells—just like the vital elements in the skin of any healthy girl of 18, has been discovered by a famous Doctor. This extract, called "Biocel," is now contained in Tokalon Rose Skinfood. Apply it every night. Every minute while you sleep your skin absorbs these vital elements. Every morning when you wake up your skin is clearer, fresher, smoother—YOUNGER. During the day use Crème Tokalon White (vanishing non-greasy). By this simple treatment any woman can make herself look ten years younger. Have a marvellous skin and complexion of which any young girl would be proud. Do not confuse Crème Tokalon with ordinary face creams which contain no skinfood ingredients. With Crème Tokalon Skinfoods successful results are positively guaranteed or money refunded.

By special arrangement any woman reader of this paper may obtain a de luxe Beauty Outfit containing new Tokalon Skinfood Creams—Rose for the night, White for the day. It also contains a special box of Poudre Tokalon and six samples of latest Paris shades. Send 3d. in stamps to cover cost of postage, packing, etc., to Tokalon Ltd. (Dept. **666W**), Chase Road, London, N.W.10.

Fashion quickly adapted to wartime conditions, as these two advertisements and an article from The Lady *magazine of 5 October clearly show.*

The Government's campaign to urge women to 'Make Do and Mend' in the new conditions of austerity was spearheaded by posters such as the one shown here; (Above) booklets full of useful tips and advice were also distributed.

In order to help women extend the life of their clothes, the Board of Trade began publishing information pamphlets such as the example which is illustrated here, *Make Do and Mend*, which contained washing and ironing tips, how to renovate old items, and the best manner of unpicking old woollen clothes and knitting them up again into new garments. Knitting, in fact, quickly became one of the most popular activities among women of all ages, according to contemporary reports. 'Of all the ways in which the nation's housewives helped their absent menfolk the most universal was knitting,' historian Norman Longmate was to write later. 'Small girls, busy mothers, even gallant grannies with arthritic fingers, all knitted. The clicking of needles could be heard constantly; people knitted in the home, in the cinema, on buses, in queues, in the air-raid shelter . . .'

In the early days of the war there was no shortage of cosmetics – with the exception of imported perfumes – though a feeling did grow throughout the country that too much make-up as well as ostentatious hairstyles were unpatriotic things for women to sport in these days of austerity. In fact, hairstyles in general became a problem in the autumn of 1939 when that most essential of hair grips, the steel kirbygrip, disappeared completely from shops, the basic raw material being otherwise required. (Hairdressers, though, continued to flourish throughout the war, particularly those who were skilled at the permanent wave.)

A far more important shortage that would soon affect every woman with a household to run was that of food – and right from the start of the war the idea of rationing commodities was one that was fiercely debated be many politicians, in particular those of the Labour Party. The argument was largely based on the fact that a high proportion of the country's food was imported – though Conservative MPs were generally opposed to any form of controls for fear that Germany

A selection of the ingenious containers manufactured to make the gas mask more stylish! (From the Illustrated London News *of 7 October 1939)*

LE DERNIER CRI IN GAS-MASK CONTAINERS: A VARIETY OF STYLES.

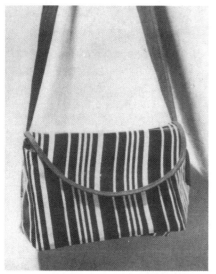

The Knitting Nuisance

The Comforts for the Services Campaign has launched a new social pest on the community —the woman who is learning to knit. It is notoriously difficult to control the arms and hands in a new and intricate operation, but that does not excuse a wild flailing of the arms and a piston-like drive of the elbows by some of these charming enthusiasts. This may be all very well in the home, where the worst she can do is to break a few mantelpiece ornaments, but in a fairly crowded railway compartment, it is intolerable. I remember observing in Switzerland that the women used a scarcely perceptible nibbling technique right at the end of the needles. There was scarcely any movement of the arms. It looked very demure, and was doubtless effective.

Kenneth Stinson,
*Ladbrooke Grove, W.*11.

The knitting craze hits wartime Britain! The reader's letter is from Picture Post.

might be able to present such a measure as propaganda exposing a 'starving Britain'. The *Daily Express*, indeed, conducted a vigorous campaign, 'Stop Rationing!', which it later claimed postponed the introduction by several months.

In fact, although rationing was not introduced until 8 January 1940, following a National Registration which began on 19 September and the issuing of ration books in October, many housewives had already begun to conserve food and make what they had go further with added titbits. (As a matter of record, the first items rationed were: butter, 4 ounces per person per week; sugar, 12 ounces; and bacon or ham, 4 ounces.)

Enter the Ministry of Food which, after a disastrous decision in early September to decentralize Billingsgate as the centre of fish distribution resulted in piles of rotting fish at depots all over the country, then played

Are you Mrs. Feckless or Mrs. Careful?

WHEN Mrs. Feckless comes to the door she often looks as if there was something burning in the oven. There often is. When Mrs. Careful comes to the door she looks as cool and immaculate as one of the daisies growing by the path. The forks at Mrs. Feckless' house sometimes taste of onion. Mrs. Careful's never do.

Being a clever housewife like Mrs. Careful means that you take your profession seriously. It's a profession in which you've got to be a cook, nurse, accountant, diplomat, plumber, gardener and sempstress. And last, but not least, a woman to whom it's still exciting to be married. And that is the reason why of "Housewife."

Between the covers of "Housewife" you will find all the sound advice, helpful hints, and inside information necessary to the smooth running of a home. "Housewife" gives full measure, and brimming over, of common sense. It's as full of interest as your own life story. Articles, competitions. Get this month's issue.

Conserving everything from food to bones and newspapers became a vital part of the war effort, as these newspaper advertisements and photograph underline. The member of the WVS collecting from this London housewife is actually a duchess!

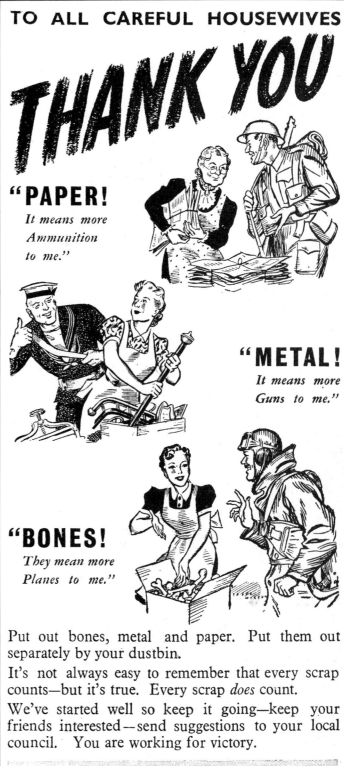

TO ALL CAREFUL HOUSEWIVES

THANK YOU

"PAPER!
It means more Ammunition to me."

"METAL!
It means more Guns to me."

"BONES!
They mean more Planes to me."

Put out bones, metal and paper. Put them out separately by your dustbin.

It's not always easy to remember that every scrap counts—but it's true. Every scrap *does* count.

We've started well so keep it going—keep your friends interested—send suggestions to your local council. You are working for victory.

"UP HOUSEWIVES AND AT 'EM!"

ISSUED BY THE MINISTRY OF SUPPLY

'Dr Carrot' and 'Potato Pete', two of the popular characters created by the Ministry of Food for their nutrition campaign.

an important role in what it called 'food control'. Without any doubt the campaign which it initiated under the title of 'The Kitchen Front' influenced as well as encouraged a great many housewives through times of scarcity. The motto of the Front was, 'Food is a munition of war – don't waste it' and among the comestibles it especially promoted were garden-grown vegetables such as carrots and potatoes. Indeed, two characters, Dr Carrot and Potato Pete, appeared everywhere in advertisements – though what actually earned carrots their popularity was the Ministry's carefully promoted story that they enabled people to see better in the dark! This message was later reinforced with tales that the most successful RAF fighter pilots lived on a diet of carrots! In fact, what enabled them to find and shoot down enemy planes at night was radar, a secret that was well kept until the end of the war.

The Kitchen Front was also promoted by a radio programme of the same title broadcast every morning directly after the eight o'clock news and which became essential listening for thrifty housewives. Following the lead of the radio, many newspapers and magazines also began to make a feature of recipes that encouraged the economic and effective use of food, and a number of typical recipes from the early days of the war are reproduced in these pages.

Less typical ideas were to be found in the pages of publications as diverse as the *Sunday Times* and *Horse & Hound* magazine. The Sunday newspaper's readers, for instance, were forthcoming with a whole variety of 'alternative' meals such as hot pea-pod soup, vegetable mould, soya bean loaf, potato and chocolate pudding, and nettle toast made, it was said, from grilling a mixture of an egg, a rasher of bacon, two slices of toasted bread and a 'pile of well-strained and seasoned nettles'! A reader of the *Church Times* also recommended eating the large beefsteak mushroom which, he claimed, when cooked 'looked and tasted like meat', while *Horse & Hound* proposed the making of cheese from sows' milk! In the columns of *The Times*, housewives were urged to try serving young bracken tips which apparently tasted like asparagus, or alternatively boiling sorrel which, a reader stoutly maintained, had the flavour of spinach.

The problem of food was compounded, of course, in that from the very first days of the war, quite a large percentage of housewives not only had their own families to feed but the evacuee mothers and children who had been billeted with them.

Despite all the upheaval, however, the everyday life of a great many women continued after the declaration of war, albeit somewhat changed. The daily shopping still had to be done (though queueing was now the

CARROTS
keep you healthy and help you
to see in the blackout

norm rather than the exception), housework demanded the same elbow-grease (though it did require new skills to cope with the exigencies of the blackout) and there were still the children to look after (those who were at home, that is).

Petrol rationing was to have an immediate effect on keeping in contact with relatives and friends – naturally closing the social circle in which women could move – but instead the emergency brought together many neighbours who had scarcely spoken to each other for years. In the space of the first week, the Mass Observation Unit was to report later, Britain had become a genuinely friendlier society than it had been since the days of the First World War when a similar threat of catastrophe had embraced the nation.

Among the better off, life also continued for a time basically unchanged from the norm, as the gossip columns of the national newspapers and society magazines bear witness. One of *Country Life*'s writers, for example, noted on 5 September:

'A scrappy, good-humoured social life begins to stir again in war-shaded, war-muffled London. In place of the *thé dansant* which suddenly began to thrive in 1914 as part of the attempts to keep men on leave continually amused we have the *cocktail dansant*, but now the young women dancing are often themselves in uniform. Dancing is spirited and an air of pleasure replaces the indifference of a few weeks ago. This may be largely due to the fact that there is now plenty of room on the dancing floors. The men's uniforms are very mixed, privates no longer avoiding the leisure-haunts of officers, and the up-to-date young officer is as un-Ouida-ish as can be – which apparently is all right with the up-to-date young woman.

'The foremost hotels and restaurants have now made their blackout and air-raid shelter provisions. It is odd to find rows of gilt chairs in the underground apartments of places like the Dorchester. Various distractions have been thought out for those taking cover. One *maître d'hôtel* says that chewing gum goes very well! Only a small minority of diners in public places have been in evening dress, but there is a growing feeling that if one goes out to such places at all it is better to dress formally, especially if one's escort wears an imposing uniform. The fluffy and crinolined dresses have been killed by their unsuitability for these queer times, but at the Hartnell and other shows there were many evening dresses of an appropriate sort – decorative without being frivolous, enveloping in cut but bright in colour.'

Social life going on much as before was also the message of *Town & Country* magazine columnist, E. H. 'London is not the deserted village some would wish it to be considered,' she wrote on 7 September. 'People are still spending a night or so there on their way back from Scotland to the country, or vice-versa. Brides have shopping to do for their new homes, whether they are to be in the country or not.'

Many of the women's organizations in towns and villages continued to meet as before, though now they set

'Home Front' and 'Kitchen Front' went hand in hand in advertisements such as these throughout the war.

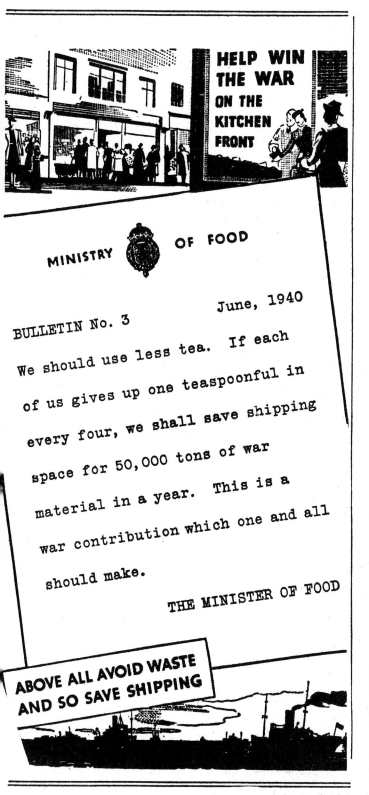

MINISTRY OF FOOD

BULLETIN No. 3 June, 1940

We should use less tea. If each of us gives up one teaspoonful in every four, we shall save shipping space for 50,000 tons of war material in a year. This is a war contribution which one and all should make.

THE MINISTER OF FOOD

ABOVE ALL AVOID WASTE AND SO SAVE SHIPPING

themselves new objectives. The Women's Institute, as one of the foremost of these with something like 332,000 members in branches throughout the country, became a 'veritable hive of industry with knitting circles, make do and mend, weaving and other rural crafts, making jam, practising home economy and taking instruction in cooking' to quote the WI's official history. With many of their husbands away from home, the members also learned to carry out such tasks as mending fuses, putting new washers on taps, and the whole variety of other domestic chores usually entrusted to the man of the house. These women also took up gardening in a big way, taking instruction in the rudiments of horticulture from local experts and generously sharing their plants and seeds around among one another. Many of the country branches even ran their own weekly markets in their WI halls, buying and selling the produce of their gardens.

Unquestionably, though, the biggest change in the lives of the women of Britain occurred right in the home. For now Britain had become a nation that stayed indoors at night. The primary cause of this was, of course, the blackout. 'The whole structure of British leisure is being changed by the blackout,' the Mass Observation Unit reported just a few weeks into the war. 'Whereas there was an increasing tendency for people to go out of their home, drawn by the ever-increasing vested interests of entertainment, this tendency has now been reversed. People are being forced to amuse themselves more, rather than sit and passively watch others do something.'

As a result of its researches, the Unit released a fascinating list of what the people of wartime Britain now considered their eight favourite activities:

1 Staying in
2 Reading
3 Going to bed early
4 Listening to the wireless
5 Going to pubs
6 Playing cards and other games
7 Writing
8 Smoking

Of particular interest among these conclusions was the fact that the first three activities scored a much higher vote than any of the others – and that among women, twice as many of them as men said that they went to bed early and that there had been no significant increase among their sex in smoking at home.

'Home life has gained a new importance,' the Unit concluded. 'A new homeliness has arisen in which our womenfolk are at the centre, providing the inspiration for our ultimate victory.'

THE SHOPPER
IN WAR-TIME

ALREADY the London shops have settled down to providing the goods women want in war-time; warm clothes, sensible shoes, overalls and equipment, inexpensive furnishings for evacuees and hostesses whose resources are suddenly taxed to the utmost. 'Business as usual' is the slogan everywhere, and there is even a certain element of fun in making one's way into the shops over little plank bridges which surmount the piles of sandbags.

AT Gamages in Holborn there is a grand selection of dark shades for your lights; washable blue celluloid for the bathroom at 2s. 11d., black or grey metal with clip-on bases for complete darkening at 1s. 11d., grander ones for important rooms. Gamages have, too, a sale of knitting-wool, and you should lay in stocks as prices are bound to rise. There are good wools for as little as 3d. an ounce and a grand tweedy bouclé wool at 5d. an ounce.

AT John Barkers, in Kensington High Street, suits of corduroy coat and breeches for the land-worker cost 45s. complete, or the breeches separately 16s. 11d. a pair. Double-breasted khaki dust-coats are 12s. 6d. each. Cross-over overalls specially designed for A.R.P. workers are 5s. 11d., or in big sizes 6s. 6d.

Their household linen department has unbleached cotton sheets at 5s. a pair, 80 by 104 inches; bleached cotton sheets are 12s. 11d. a pair; warm reversible plaid rugs at 5s. each. And their woollen department has a special sale of genuine handwoven Harris tweeds, 28 to 30 inches wide, at 3s. 6d. a yard; this is undoubtedly the time to have a classic suit tailored in the hardest-wearing material known.

A PADDED and quilted material called 'Quiltette' is sold by the yard at D. H. Evans, 2s. 11½d. a yard, 34 inches wide. It is made in pale chintzy patterns and in dark ones, and would be admirable for making up your own warm house-coat, bed-jacket, bed quilts or cot covers at small expense. This shop has a big stock of patterns in Nursery Viyella and Clydella for warm, easily laundered children's clothes.

FELTING for your gasproof room, 54 inches wide, costs 2s. 6½d. at John Lewis, Oxford Street; and a special rubberised felt is 3s. 11d. Their household linen department has very good, light, down-filled quilts in printed cambric at 12s. 11d.

From *The Lady*, 9 September 1939

"Oh, dear, I hope I'm not spending all this money for nothing."

*Time and Tide,
2 September 1939*

Wartime Recipes

By exchanging knowledge and experience, cooks can help one another to tide over this difficult period. Everywhere ladies have shown their willingness to help, not only by sending in first-class wartime recipes to the newspapers and 'The Kitchen Front', but also by their response to requests – like the one made last week for a method of preserving fats.

Preserving Fats

The following simple and reliable method of preserving fats has been sent in, with occasional slight variations, by a number of people:
Cut up the fat into small pieces, put in a saucepan and leave over a very gentle heat until it has all melted. Have ready clean, well-heated jars, stand them on a hot, damp cloth, and strain the melted fat into them. Cover, when cold, with cotton fabric dipped in melted wax or with jam-pot covers. It will keep for many months in a cool, dry place.

Beetroot Soup

Ingredients: 2 beetroots, small head of celery, one pint and a half of water or vegetable stock.
Bake the beetroots, peel and chop them up with the head of celery. Cook these with the water or stock, adding a tablespoonful of vinegar to taste. Cook until soft enough to squeeze through a sieve. Thicken with a little flour and fat and season to taste.

Potato and Tomato Pie

Ingredients: 1 lb cold or par-boiled potatoes, ½ lb tomatoes, small onion (finely chopped), teaspoonful finely chopped parsley, pepper and salt to taste, dessertspoonful flour, ½ pint milk, 2 oz grated cheese.
Cut potatoes and tomatoes in thick slices and arrange in layers in a pie-dish. Sprinkle a little onion and parsley on each layer, also pepper and salt. Put flour in a saucepan, mix smoothly with a little milk, add the rest (previously warmed) and stir until it boils. Add half the grated cheese and pour it over the potatoes and tomatoes. Sprinkle the rest of the cheese on top and bake in a moderate hot oven for about half an hour.

Oatmeal Sausages

Ingredients: 2 oz chopped meat, 2 tablespoonful chopped onion, ½ oz cooking fat, 4 oz oatmeal, ½ pint water, 2 teaspoonful salt, pinch of pepper, browned breadcrumbs.
First fry the onion in the cooking fat until it is lightly browned. Stir in the oatmeal, adding the water and bring to the boil, stirring all the time. Cook for 10 to 15 minutes, stirring regularly. Add the chopped meat and seasoning, mixing well and then spread on a plate to cool. This will divide into eight portions which can be rolled into sausage shapes, after which coat lightly with the browned breadcrumbs and grill lightly.

Eggless Cake

Ingredients: 1 lb flour, 3 ozs sugar, 4 ozs margarine, 4 ozs of raisins, a little mixed spice or ginger, a teaspoonful of bicarbonate of soda, half a pint of milk, teaspoonful of vinegar.
Cream the margarine and sugar. Dissolve the bicarbonate of soda in the milk, and add this alternately with the flour and fruit to the creamed margarine, beating all the time. Leave the mixture for approximately one hour to rise. Then add the vinegar, and bake in a lined and covered tin for one and a half hours in a moderate oven.

Sugarless Sweet

A most delicious sweet course can be made by mashing up stewed apples and using them instead of water with a packet of orange jelly. The apples can be varied with many other flavours of jelly, the most popular combinations after orange being lemon and greengage.

Baking-Powder Rolls

Ingredients: 1 lb plain flour, 2 teaspoonfuls baking powder, teaspoonful salt, milk and water.
Sieve together the plain flour, baking powder and salt, and mix this into a dough using the milk and water. Knead the mixture lightly and then roll it out to approximately three-quarters of an inch in thickness. Cut into rounds and shape these into rolls. Brush with a little milk and then bake the rolls in a hot oven for 20 minutes.

Carrot Jam

Ingredients: 8 oz carrots, 1 lb cooking apples, 1 lb sugar.
This delicious jam can be made when fruits are not available. First peel and cook the carrots in a little water. Then slice the apples and cook in one-quarter of a pint of water until a smooth pulp. Mix the carrots and apples together, and for each one pint measure add 1 lb of sugar. Return the mixture to the saucepan and continue stirring until the sugar has dissolved. Boil the jam until it has stiffened.

Air-Raid Provisions

Finally, a word on some items to take into the air-raid shelter when the siren goes as there is no telling how long you may have to stay there. Don't forget some fresh drinking water, though hot tea or coffee in a flask can be very welcome when you are dry. A bar of chocolate makes a good snack, as well as dried fruits like sultanas, raisins or figs. Barley sugar and boiled sweets are also excellent stand-bys, and so is chewing gum. Ideal, too, are oranges which can quench your thirst and stave off the hunger pains!

September 1939.

7 Digging for Victory

Britain's legions of gardeners were swiftly recruited into the action when war was declared. 'Dig For Victory!' was a phrase coined by the Minister of Agriculture, Sir Reginald Dorman-Smith, to urge every gardener, allotment holder and possessor of a smallholding to produce more from their land – and dig to very considerable effect they all certainly did!

The people of the United Kingdom have for generations been enthusiastic gardeners, finding pleasure and relaxation – not to mention supplementary crops of vegetables for their larders! – from the devoted tending of their little plots of earth. The topic of gardening had also long been a popular feature in newspapers, magazines and on the radio, and the nation in September 1939 possessed a number of well-known pundits such as C. H. Middleton and W. Beach Thomas.

IF SWORDS WERE PLOUGHSHARES . . .

September brought, as often, the loveliest weather of the year. All the proper symptoms of the date are at the highest power. Growth is of almost fantastic speed in bushes so different as the rose and the yew. The apple trees grow, while their abundant fruit is maturing. Grass has hardly grown so fast all the year. The robin sings from dawn to dusk and after. The martins and swallows cluster, but are loth to leave. Did so many meadow-brown butterflies ever appear before in one week? The bees still make honey. If only swords were ploughshares, for it was perfect farmers' weather!

From *Country Life*, 15 September 1939

It was actually a broadcast to the nation by Sir Reginald which initiated all the feverish activity, and his campaign to grow more food became almost an obsession among many of those people not directly involved in the war. Speaking on the radio, the Minister had declared, 'Half a million more allotments properly worked will provide potatoes and vegetables that will feed another million adults and one and a half million children for eight months out of the twelve. So let "Dig For Victory" be the motto of everyone with a garden and of every able-bodied man and woman capable of digging an allotment in their spare time.'

Sir Reginald's Ministry also immediately initiated a campaign to encourage publishers to produce books about horticulture which would explain how even the newest gardener could generate green fingers. 'Books can help you dig for victory,' the Ministry enthused.

Another powerful medium in this campaign was the weekly magazine *The Smallholder*, which became a mine of information supplied by experts and added to by the personal experiences of amateur gardeners. This publication was undoubtedly worth its weight in gold to many hard-pressed families in helping them to augment their diets in the midst of rationing.

One immediate response among the more enthusiastic of the nation's gardeners was to dig up their lawns and flower beds and turn them into vegetable patches! This lead was also followed by some local authorities – a number of Kent councils, for instance, growing potatoes and vegetables in their parks and on grass verges! Even in the cities there were people who turned their window boxes into miniature vegetable patches, with runner beans and tomatoes as the most favoured crops!

Local horticultural and allotment societies also sprang up all over the country, and where those anxious to cultivate the soil could find nowhere easily to hand, they turned instead to waste land and even rubbish tips – often with the most unexpected and successful results!

C. H. Middleton, who wisely counselled many of these amateur enthusiasts, said later, 'Though there is no doubt the farmers played a big part in providing enough food for the people during the war, I am sure that without the gardeners and allotment holders there were families who would have gone hungry. Many of these gardeners were very ingenious, too. They managed to get a tremendous number of crops into small spaces and then protected them fiercely from the birds. I sometimes think the birds had a tougher war than human beings!'

Middleton's colleague, W. Beach Thomas, was the gardening broadcaster who did much to encourage the people of Britain also to raise rabbits and chickens in their gardens as a further source of food. His campaigning, in fact, helped to make the Government lift its previous restrictions against the keeping of poultry and rabbits in domestic gardens. Beach Thomas's weekly radio talks 'In the Garden' were peppered with sound advice and the odd touch of humour, as this typical extract from his broadcast of 15 September 1939 will demonstrate.

'Dig for Victory' – one of the most effective and best remembered posters of the Second World War.

DIG FOR VICTORY

*Gardeners young and old set to work as Britain goes
to war. (Above) Women are lending a hand to dig an
allotment in a London park, while (opposite) three
evacuated city children prepare for work in the
country.*

'We are all urged to grow more vegetables, and this may actually be done in many places without destroying flower gardens or bringing much new land into cultivation. It has been recently demonstrated that a glasshouse about a yard square and seven feet high can provide food for half a dozen cows or scores of poultry for many weeks, by the sprouting of maize on electrically heated trays. We cannot emulate this scientific feat, but all who possess any sort of glasshouse can grow much good food in shallow trays. Early potatoes so grown are a great luxury and good food to boot.

'Many other vegetables may be sprouted in the house, and like sweet peas, so treated, they will come into bearing at a very much earlier date than crops sown out of doors. One of the vegetables worth sowing out of doors in autumn is the broad bean. The venture is a risk worth taking in any bigger garden.'

Turning to the increasingly vital topic of the 'keeping qualities' of vegetables, Mr Beach Thomas said this depended very much on the manner of their treatment. 'Onions, for example,' he said, 'keep very much better if the earth is cleared away from the bulb when it has virtually finished its growth. The most decorative vegetable, and one of the most useful, is the carrot. It makes – to quote one instance I have observed recently – a quite attractive fringe to the strip of earth often left outside the wire of a hard tennis court. To such odd places the short-rooted varieties are better suited than the long.'

Apart from chickens and rabbits, quite a considerable number of people who had the necessary space took to keeping other livestock. Some opted for goats, which were easy to feed, being quite content with greens – although not above partaking of any newspapers or items of clothing foolishly left within their reach! Others chose cows, one of which on a small-holding could quite happily keep a family in milk and butter; while a smaller number reared pigs, sometimes in groups known as Pig Clubs, which consisted of several families who would all share in the resulting rashers!

The war, of course, radically changed the status of the farmer. Now his produce was almost as vital to the nation as that of the munitions maker, and the Ministry of Agriculture set about urging all farmers to extract the maximum amount of crops from their acres. And because the amount of arable land had declined to just nine million acres in 1939 from a high of eleven million acres just twenty years earlier, there was plenty lying fallow. Monetary encouragement was offered for the ploughing of new land (£2 for every acre) and directives went out (not always well received) as to what the farmers were to grow.

Though these men may have grumbled at many of

The poster appeal for people to 'Keep a Pig!' resulted in Pig Clubs such as that run by the Hyde Park Police!

the demands put upon them, their response to the call was excellent, and their contribution proved vital to the war effort, as is shown by the fact that in 1939 the country was importing two-thirds of its food and by the end just one-third. The kudos aside, these productive folk also had more than enough meat, eggs, bacon, butter and cheese on their own tables to make rationing something quite foreign to their families.

Because the call-up had taken men away from the countryside just as it had done in the towns, the

farmers required help from other sources. Youngsters not old enough for service were an obvious choice, and great numbers of boys and girls answered the 'Help the Farmer' scheme which came into being at the start of September. And along with them came the famous Women's Land Army.

The Army had been set up with considerable foresight in June 1939 so that should war come – as it did – then volunteer women, most from the towns and cities, would be ready for work on the farms of Britain. And although these 'Land Girls', as they were more familiarly called, may have been initially regarded with some wariness by the farmers (and probably even more so by their wives!) in the vast majority of cases they proved themselves keen to learn, hard-working and eternally cheerful.

The girls – particularly the pretty ones – proved ideal photographic material for the newspapers, a fact which has tended rather to glamorize all of them and their work which was often dirty, back-breaking, lasted from dawn until dusk and on average earned them a paltry 28 shillings a week! Suggestions that the girls were inclined to be of rather loose morals are difficult to substantiate, and seem to have emanated from country girls disgruntled with their new rivals from the towns. A story that the motto of Land Girls was 'Backs to the Land' is certainly without any foundation!

Despite such slanders and the fact that they were often poorly clothed for the conditions in which they had to work, almost 90,000 females between the ages of eighteen and forty served in the Women's Land Army during the war years. For many, too, it was a satisfying experience that nothing would ever diminish. Mrs Doris Jones, who was born in London but later married and settled in Northampton where she had served for five years as a Land Girl, speaks for the vast majority of her colleagues when she says:

'A lot of people thought we were a bit of a joke to start with – city girls playing at being milk-maids and shepherdesses. And with those breeches that didn't fit, the wellington boots that were too big, and those silly felt hats, I suppose we *were* a sight. But we all had a tremendous sense of purpose and we loved looking after the animals.

'In time, most of us got to know quite a lot about the land and about farming, and I am sure you can find plenty of farmers who will tell you they owe a good deal to the Land Girls. On the farm where I worked, the farmer said we were the best help he had ever had – and I can assure you he was a taciturn chap not given to easily praising anything or anyone! It was undoubtedly one of the most fulfilling and happiest times of my life,' Mrs Jones adds, with more than a trace of wistfulness in her voice.

An appeal by the Ministry of Agriculture for greater effort from the nation's farmers.

A Ministry of Agriculture appeal

Women and girls were recruited to work in agriculture and formed the famous Women's Land Army.

For a healthy, happy job

Join the

WOMEN'S LAND ARMY

For details:

APPLY TO NEAREST W.L.A. COUNTY OFFICE OR TO W.L.A. HEADQUARTERS 6 CHESHAM ~~PLACE~~ LONDON S.W. STREET

Issued by the Ministry of Agriculture and the Ministry of Labour and National Service

The glamorized view of the Land Girl as presented on the cover of Lilliput magazine – and closer to reality.

Lilliput

ONE SHILLING

APRIL 1943

Trier

Just one of the many perils motorists faced on the roads of wartime Britain – here a driver encounters a Home Guard wire barricade and smoke screen!

8 Motoring the Feather-Weight Way

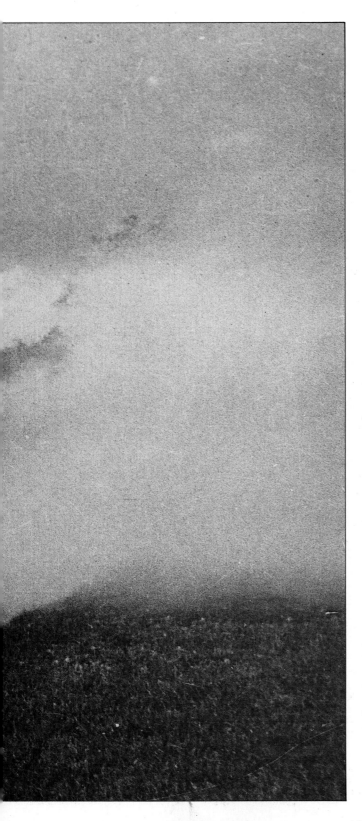

The impact of the war was to be swift and far-reaching on the life of the British motorist. Though there were by no means as many cars on the roads at the start of September 1939 as there are today – the official figure was 2,000,000 – Mr and Mrs Britain were growing ever more dependent on their motor vehicles, a fact well reflected in a column by 'Janus' in *The Spectator* of 15 September:

'In the country, much more, no doubt than in the towns, there is now a general and soul-searching review of tasks to be done and people to be seen "before the petrol goes". Friends who will soon be out of reach must be visited or asked over; the last visit to the cinema must be paid by those who follow films; or the last visit to the hairdresser by those concerned with coiffures.

'It is too soon to realise yet what life in the village will mean without petrol. In the last war private cars were comparatively rare. Today, in the country at any rate, all life is based on them. People build houses in remote spots they would never have thought of without a car to maintain communications. Many of them will be virtually marooned. Social life, too, will be enormously restricted. Hitherto anyone within thirty miles or so was well within the circle. Now the radius will shrink to about two, and to people employed in the day to nothing at all, for no one is going to drive unnecessarily after dark, even if he has petrol to spare. We shall be thrown completely in on ourselves; that may be good or bad.'

'Janus', as it transpired, had good reason to be apprehensive about the future for the British motorist.

Despite all the anxieties in the world during the summer months, the motor trade had been as busy as ever promoting its new lines for the autumn, and even in the last week of August, major manufacturers like Vauxhall were claiming 'Better Motoring for 1940' with PRICES DOWN for their range of cars from the 10 h.p. model costing £159 to the top of the class 25 h.p. De Luxe Saloon 'built to meet world competition' at £330! (See advertisement reproduced on page 96.)

Second-hand car dealers were also to enjoy something of a boom in sales, if only for a comparatively short period of time. For with the switching of much of the manufacturing industry to making munitions, private cars shortly ceased to roll from the production lines of Ford, Rover, Morris, Rolls Royce and all the other companies. (In fact, making cars did not cease completely until October 1940, though after July of that year it was illegal to buy a new car without a licence – which would certainly *not* have been granted for a private vehicle.) Demand therefore rose for second-hand cars, and in the first year of the war it was not at all unusual for two- and three-year-old models to be

Better Motoring
for 1940 . . yet
PRICES DOWN

		FROM
10 h.p.	The Roomiest "Ten" you can buy. Wider; longer; smarter; 60 m.p.h. 40 m.p.g. with normal driving.	**£159**
12 h.p.	Best "Twelve" — Lowest Price. Incomparable value; smarter frontal appearance; more room. 65 m.p.h., 35 m.p.g. with normal driving.	**£185**
14 h.p.	Most Famous "Fourteen" in the World. Much more luxurious interior. 70 m.p.h. 30 m.p.g. with normal driving.	**£220**
25 h.p.	Built to meet World Competition. Extremely luxurious finish and appointments. 80 m.p.h., 20 m.p.g. with normal driving.	**£330**

Every Vauxhall combines all these seven practical features. **1.** *ECONOMY.* Low purchase price, 20% more m.p.g. Low maintenance costs. **2.** *OUTSTANDING PERFORMANCE.* High average speed, smooth O.H.V. power output. **3.** *THE SMOOTHEST RIDE ON WHEELS.* Vauxhall Independent Suspension smooths all roads. **4.** *REAL DRIVING EASE.* Good vision, handy effortless controls. Controlled Synchro-mesh gear change. **5.** *CONSTANT SAFETY.* Powerful Hydraulic brakes. Great strength and rigidity with integral body construction on latest models. **6.** *ROOMY COMFORT.* Generous seating room and luggage space. **7.** *QUIETNESS.* Moving parts are really silent; sound further dampened by body insulation.

Despite big price reductions, Vauxhall cars have been still further improved for 1940.

Always, motorists have approved the Vauxhall policy of providing better motoring for less money. Now, with lower prices and *low running costs*, you can save *more* than the new extra tax whatever Vauxhall model you choose. Your motoring will be more enjoyable, more economical than ever.

Every Vauxhall is distinctively modern in appearance, outstanding in performance, safe, roomy and delightful to drive. Reliability is assured and maintenance costs are really low. *Only* Vauxhall can give you such value. *Your nearest Vauxhall dealer can give immediate delivery.* Ask him for catalogues and a trial run. Let a ride decide. Vauxhall Motors Limited, Luton, Beds.

Here is the 1940 Vauxhall "10" 4-door De Luxe Saloon **£169**

Only VAUXHALL can give you such VALUE

Two typical advertisements from September 1939. (Below) Promoting one of the most popular cars on the road, the Austin Seven, and (opposite) an optimistic Vauxhall declaration of better motoring to come in 1940.

Be sure your car is made in the United Kingdom

A "VETERAN'S" ADVICE ON ECONOMICAL MOTORING

TELEGRAM

OF COURSE YOU CAN AFFORD AUSTIN SEVEN + WORTH THE EXTRA FEW POUNDS + CHEAPEST TO BUY ISN'T ALWAYS CHEAPEST TO RUN + PLAY SAFE + TRUE ECONOMY COMES FROM AUSTIN DEPENDABILITY + NEGLIGIBLE REPAIR BILLS + PENNY A MILE RUNNING COSTS + EASY TO DRIVE + SEE 1937 IMPROVEMENTS INCLUDING SOUND INSULATION + TAKES EXPERIENCE TO JUDGE VALUE + NO OFFENCE MEANT +   + DIGBY +

Experience teaches that true motoring economy lies not only in the initial cost, but in the maintenance costs involved. The dependable Austin Seven is exceptionally light on petrol, oil and tyres. Repair bills are few and far between. Running costs average less than a penny a mile for four people—less than a farthing a mile per person! This low maintenance cost, therefore, justifies a few extra pounds initial outlay.

And, remember, numerous improvements add to the appeal of the new model. There is the new engine with THREE-BEARING CRANKSHAFT which gives swifter acceleration and greater power. New GIRLING-TYPE BRAKES which respond to the slightest pressure. The new FLEXIBLE CLUTCH which engages gradually and smoothly. The smarter, roomier body which is SOUND INSULATED to ensure quiet running. Ask to try the economical Austin Seven.

AUSTIN SEVEN

Seven Prices at (works):

New Ruby Saloon - -	£125
New Ruby Fxd.-Hd Sal.	£122
New Pearl Cabriolet -	£128
Open Road Tourer -	£112
Two-Seater - - -	£102.10

Have you seen the Austin Magazine for May?

You buy a car—but you invest in an Austin

The Austin Motor Co. Ltd., Birmingham & 479 Oxford Street, London, W.1. London Service Depots : 12, 14, 18 & 20 h.p.—Holland Park, W.11. 7 & 10 h.p.—North Row, W.1. Export Dept. : Birmingham.

resold for twice and sometimes more than their original cost. Particularly in demand were the economical small cars like the famous Austin Seven and Ford Eight which then retailed at around £100 each!

The motoring public realized that hard times lay ahead as early as 9 p.m. on 3 September when BBC Radio news announced that as from the following day only one grade of petrol would be available at garages. This blend of petrol – which, it was said, would be better than the normal 'Grade 3' but not up to the standard of the 'Premium' already available from the various oil companies – was to be called 'Pool' and would cost 1s 6d per gallon. Nor was this the worst of the news. In two weeks' time, on Wednesday 16 September – the sonorous tones of the announcer declared – *rationing* of petrol would commence for all motorists!

PAID HEAVILY FOR A CAR

When Mr L. Shepherd of Weymouth sold to a customer a motor car for £60 he was paid the whole purchase price in copper coins. The vendor had to borrow the car to take away the money which was packed in paper bags!

From the *Daily Express*, 8 September 1939

This rationing would be based on the size of the driver's car: an Austin Seven, for instance, would rate four gallons per month, to a maximum of ten for the largest vehicles of 20 horse power and over such as Rolls Royces and Daimlers. It was estimated that these amounts would enable motorists to cover an average of 7 miles per day and up to 200 miles per month if used carefully. The fast or careless driver might hope to manage only as little as 100 miles. The 500,000 British motorcyclists were to be allowed just two gallons per month, and as the size of the machine would make no difference to the ration, this obviously favoured the smaller bikes.

It was perhaps no surprise to anyone that on the Tuesday morning before rationing was due to begin enormous queues of vehicles were seen outside garages across the country in towns and cities as motorists endeavoured to fill their tanks to the brim one last time. A large number of garages ran out of supplies early in the day and there were heated exchanges in many stations where the owners tried to exercise their own pre-emptive form of rationing to satisfy everyone.

In fact, the panic proved unnecessary, for that afternoon the Government announced a postponement of rationing until midnight on 22 September. When that day duly arrived, there was a much less frantic and more orderly acceptance of the restrictions. Every motorist was issued with a 'Motor Spirit Ration Book' (see illustration) from which the garage owner had to remove the coupons as he pumped out the allowance. Stringent new laws were also brought in to ensure that there was no black market in these coupons, and harsh penalties were introduced to prevent the storage of petrol by anyone without a licence to do so. Although there were undoubtedly people who flouted both these regulations – and others who took the illegal course of adding paraffin to their allowance to make it go further – of much greater annoyance to the average man was the 'siphoner' who took advantage of the blackout to empty the tanks of any cars left foolishly parked in the street.

There seems little doubt that the lack of petrol in the early months of the war was the most keenly felt of all the shortages – and newspapers, magazines and even the radio were quick to offer tips about the conservation of this now precious spirit. 'How to Get More Miles to the Gallon' was a title frequently encountered that September, as motoring experts recommended their audiences to keep their cars in 'perfect' running order (regularly checking their sparking plugs, carburettor and petrol pipe), to drive steadily, avoid violent braking, and to switch off the engine whenever the chance to coast in neutral presented itself. As *The Motor*'s John Prioleau summarized it: 'Keep your engine in the best condition you can, keep the fuel system and ignition system as clean as possible; and drive with feather-weight fingers and feather-weight feet.'

That motorists as a whole accepted the rationing with a good grace was due in no small measure to the comprehensive figures that were issued by the authorities to show just how much petrol it took to keep our aircraft flying and our military vehicles operational. (One operational flight of a Spitfire required the same amount of petrol that would keep a family car running for a year, it was claimed.) Radio broadcasts by such knowledgeable experts as Captain Euan Wallace also had considerable impact, and many of his talks were repeated to let the message sink in. Take this typical extract from one of his broadcasts given on 7 September:

'Do not use your car or motorcycle unnecessarily. Every vehicle which is not on the road for some definite purpose connected with our war effort is liable to hamper the movement of essential traffic, and in the case of an air raid to impede the passage of fire-fighting

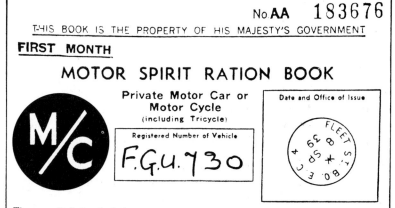

No **AA** 183676

FIRST MONTH

MOTOR SPIRIT RATION BOOK

M/C

Private Motor Car or
Motor Cycle
(including Tricycle)

Registered Number of Vehicle

F.G.U.730

Date and Office of Issue

FLEET ST.
E.C.4
8 SP 39

The issue of a Ration Book does not guarantee to the holder any minimum quantity of motor spirit and the book may be cancelled at any time without notice

This book must be surrendered with any unused coupons when application is made for a subsequent book and no such book will be issued unless this book has been surrendered.

No **AB** 183676
NOT TRANSFERABLE

This coupon is issued under the authority of the
BOARD OF TRADE

1 ONE UNIT

1. The coupons in this book authorise the holder to purchase the number of units of motor spirit specified on the coupons for use in the vehicle bearing the number shown on the front of this book and must not be used for any other purpose.

2. This book must be produced whenever motor spirit is purchased and coupons must only be detached by the supplier at the time of purchase who must also fill in the particulars required.

3. The quantity represented by a UNIT of motor spirit is subject to modification and will be officially announced from time to time.

Quantity supplied :

.... Gallons.

Name of Supplier :

....

Date ....

Note —Motor Spirit must only be supplied into the tank of the vehicle bearing the number shown on the front of this book and must not be supplied into any other container

One of the millions of petrol rationing books issued in September 1939; and (below) a typically humorous Punch *cartoon on the subject of rationing.*

"Couldn't we economise on petrol by not using all the horse-power, Murphy?"

Poster issued to help motorists prepare their vehicles for night-time driving.

vehicles and ambulances. All users of the road should make it a point of honour to study and obey all regulations and instructions which affect them, and to carry out at once and without question directions given to them by the police or wardens. If you *have* to use a car, be ready to give people a lift.

'There is likely to be congestion on the public passenger services, for instance when the "All Clear" signal is given after an air-raid warning. You can be particularly helpful in the rush hours. Remember that large numbers of children have been moved from urban centres into the country districts so that they will be less exposed to the dangers of the war; and keep a special lookout for children on the roads in the country.'

Captain Wallace then turned to the dramatic changes in night-time driving which had followed the introduction of blackout regulations. Motorists were to be treated no differently to anyone else in the matter of concealing their lights.

'Those of us who have been obliged to drive at night have found conditions difficult,' he said with creditable understatement. 'Pedestrians can do a lot to help, and incidentally save accidents to themselves, by observing these four simple rules. Firstly, always use marked crossings if you can; and at cross-roads where there is a control either by the police or by light signals, wait until the traffic is held up before you cross. Secondly, wear or carry something white at night – a handkerchief round your arm, or perhaps a newspaper – so that drivers can see you more easily. Thirdly, do not walk near the kerb with your back to the traffic; this means keeping to the left on pavements. Fourthly, if there is no footpath keep to the right so that you face oncoming traffic.

'One final word to motorists. Do not park your car at night facing the wrong way. If you do, you may easily mislead other drivers as to the line of the road and cause an accident. Above all, remember that blackout conditions mean that we must *all* go slow!'

An ARP ambulance after being adapted for the new wartime conditions – complete with specially-hooded headlamps and white bumper and mudguards.

Captain Wallace was right to be concerned about the risk of accidents, for despite all the regulations concerning the use of cars, the death toll on the roads of Britain for the months of September to December 1939 almost doubled over the previous year's. In the corresponding months of 1938, 2494 people had been killed; in the last quarter of 1939 the figure reached a horrifying 4133. It was a tragic thing to have to report, but more people died on the country's roads during that time than were killed on active service.

CYCLISTS' LIGHTS

Adolf Hitler has, no doubt quite unintentionally, done us one good turn. He has compelled us to bring forth a law which provides that every pedal cycle shall carry a rear red light at night. The death and casualty list of road accidents will surely be reduced by the introduction of this belated measure, and incidentally, we shall cease to be the only nation in the world foolish enough to allow such an absurd state of things to exist against all the exigencies of common sense.

A letter from Sir George Roberts in *The Times*, 9 September 1939

There is little doubt that many motorists still drove too fast for the conditions and with little regard for the fact that everyone now had the minimum of lighting. Car headlamps had, in fact, to be covered by a disc of cardboard with a small half-moon shape cut into the middle (these were replaced by a rather more effective mask with three horizontal slits early in 1940), while side-lights and rear lamps were covered by sheets of tissue paper. Reflectors had to be blackened. The one exception to these restrictions was during a heavy fog when it was presumed everything on the ground was invisible to any raiders above.

All vehicles had to have a streak of white paint right around the body, including the running board, across the mudguards and over the bumpers. And interior lights, including those on the dashboard, were banned. Radios were similarly forbidden, and a little later it also became a punishable offence not to immobilize a car parked anywhere but in a locked garage!

But despite all these precautions, the accident figures still continued to rise over the winter of 1939, and in February 1940 a new speed limit of 20 miles per hour was introduced for all built-up areas. Protests from careful motorists and some of the motoring organizations received no sympathy from the Government, appalled as MPs were by the death toll. Even some ingenious alternative ideas failed to move the Minister of Transport – including one quite amazing suggestion that motorists might drive on the *opposite* side of the road at night so that the driver could navigate by the white-painted kerbs! (Incidentally, the now familiar white lines down the centre of the road were actually a welcome innovation for which we can all thank a later period of the war.)

Curious as it may seem amidst all this carnage, the driving test was suspended at the outbreak of the war, and learner drivers merely had to apply for a 'National Service Licence'. Thereafter they were free to take to the roads without even an experienced driver as a passenger or displaying 'L' plates!

In time, the petrol rationing (which underwent further restrictions and then, in July 1942, all allowances for pleasure motoring were withdrawn by the Government) and the general wear and tear on vehicles (not forgetting the increasing difficulty owners had in getting spare parts and someone to fit them) caused a dramatic decline in private motoring in Britain. According to official figures, only 700,000 private cars were licensed in January 1944, and at the end of the war this figure was scarcely half a million.

A great many vehicles were undoubtedly just driven to death during these wartime years or else fell apart through age and lack of care. Some of the more car-proud motorists gave up the struggle and simply laid their vehicles up on blocks in their garages. None of these people, though, was to derive quite as pleasant a benefit as a result of this exercise as did Sir William Lyons, the founder of Jaguar cars, when he uncovered his pride and joy after the hostilities were over.

The apple of his eye was a brand-new two and a half litre SS100, which he put under wraps on the very day war was declared and left mothballed until 1947. Then, as a promotional exercise, Sir William had the car fitted out with a new three and a half litre engine and entered it in the Monte Carlo rally that year and the Coupe des Alpes in 1948. Thereafter, for its help in relaunching the Jaguar marque, the SS100 led a life of comfort and ease on display until it was at last put up for auction in London in February 1988. Coys, the vintage car auctioneers of Kensington, estimated that the wartime veteran would fetch between £75,000 and £85,000. In fact, the Jaguar was sold for a world-record price to a Hertfordshire businessman for . . . £165,000!

One inventive motorist found a way around petrol rationing by adapting his car to run on coal gas!

9 Travelling on the Blackout Special

On the railways of Britain, the war started in the immediate aftermath of what has long been a familiar situation – the threat of a strike! On 25 August the Associated Society of Locomotive Engineers and Firemen (ASLEF) announced that they were calling for an all-out strike of members from midnight on the following Saturday, 2 September.

At this time, there was no nationalized British Railways, although the original 250 separate companies which had grown up to cover the nation had, since 1921, consisted of just four main-line railway systems. The other major rail union, the National Union of Railwaymen (NUR), also had a claim in at this time demanding a minimum wage of 50 shillings (£2.50) per week – but this had been rejected by the four companies. The NUR, in contrast to ASLEF, who represented 56,000 of the highest-paid railwaymen all earning more than the minimum wage asked for by the NUR, was not threatening a strike but was in the process of resubmitting its claim to the Railway Staff National Tribunal. This course of action had undoubtedly earned the union considerable public sympathy during the tense week – just as that of ASLEF had brought the fury of many, in particular the press, down on them.

In a strongly worded attack, *The Spectator* spoke for many when it declared, 'While this country hovers on the brink of war, ASLEF has chosen to call a strike of its members. Nothing could exceed the folly of this decision. It will harm their country, their class, their union, and their own cause; by its abuse of the strike weapon it will weaken trade union action everywhere.

'Its only advantage is to throw into even greater relief the moderation and wisdom of the NUR who are demanding a minimum wage of 50s a week. This claim, which has wide public sympathy, has been rejected by the companies; and it has now been resubmitted by the NUR to the Railway Staff National Tribunal. Their self-restraint will increase the force of their claim.'

The Spectator believed that the only reason ASLEF was making its claim at this time on behalf of its better-paid members was that it was 'actuated by the

The railways keep on running – an evocative photograph and dramatic poster from September 1939.

A typically packed train on the day war broke out.

knowledge that in normal times they could reduce the railway communications of the country to a standstill. These, however, are not normal times; and the locomotive men will have cause to regret that at such a moment they have put their own interests before those both of the country as a whole and their fellow workers.'

In fact, on 1 September the Government, anticipating the crisis to come, took over the four railway companies as well as London Transport, guaranteeing them in return a minimum annual income, with any additional receipts being divided equally between the two parties. As it transpired, the railways of Britain were run throughout the war at a considerable profit!

However, it is true to say that services from that September weekend were thereafter continually subject to delay, scheduling difficulties and no end of inconveniences for passengers. Yet, as elsewhere in the nation, the British spirit overcame what was widely described as the 'nightmare' of travelling by train. Although hard-pressed announcers and station staff tried their best to placate passengers, placards soon began appearing to appeal to the better nature of the public: 'Food, shells and fuel must come first,' declared one widely posted bill. 'If your train is late or crowded – *do you mind?*'

Apart from the extra demands on their carrying capacity, the railways also had to contend with operating at night under the restrictions of the blackout, extinguishing all lights both on the engines and in the carriages. These curbs inevitably played havoc with timetables as well as creating new problems for passengers as they stumbled over one another, occasionally sat on each other's laps, and even wandered into the wrong toilets in the eerie darkness! The introduction in December of boxed-in lighting which threw a thin beam into each carriage did ease the problems somewhat, however.

Because stations also had to adhere to the blackout rules, finding the right platform, let alone the right train, was also something of a lottery for the travelling public in the first few days of September, as they and the railway staff came to terms with this strange new way of life. Many a man and woman using the railways at the time can still recall getting on the wrong train, disembarking at the wrong station, or simply finding themselves many miles from where they expected to be because of sudden destination or schedule changes!

There were, though, posters which appeared trying to make life easier. 'If you can't see the name and can't hear the porter's voice,' one advised travellers, 'ask another passenger.' Which was all right, of course, as long as there was someone *local* in the carriage!

If there were any compensations amidst all the overcrowding on the trains, it was that the first- and third-class seating arrangements were rarely observed and any complaints uttered were treated with universal scorn. On the subject of crowded trains, Mrs Daphne Lord, who was a civil servant in 1939 and now lives in Hertfordshire, remembers: 'On all trains every inch of space was taken up in the carriages and the corridors, and people would even perch on the loo seats. If you were lucky enough to get a seat you hung on to it for dear life! Some mothers would even put their children in the luggage racks if there were no seats, and woe betide everyone in the compartment if the child suddenly felt sick!

'I remember seeing many people sitting on the laps of others: there were certainly no shortage of offers from men to pretty young girls! Some trains got so packed that people actually had to climb in and out of the carriages through the windows. But despite the discomfort and hours of being squeezed in with other bodies, it was amazing how good-tempered everyone remained. You got to the end of a journey having made lots of new friends. Still, the simple truth of the matter then was that if you missed your train you just couldn't be sure *when* the next one might be.'

As if to emphasize to people only to travel if it was essential, all 'cheap-day returns' were immediately withdrawn, and yet another poster appeared enquiring, 'Is your journey *really* necessary?'

Sometimes unintentional humour lightened the load of frazzled passengers. In the first weeks of the war, an announcement regularly broadcast at all main-line stations would result in hoots of laughter. 'If an air raid is sounded,' a rather stentorian voice declared, 'passengers may go to the shelters or proceed by their trains. Members of the Armed Forces *must* take shelter!'

On the outbreak of war, many station buffets began to function erratically due to lack of food or crockery, and all restaurant cars were taken out of service – not only depriving the public of any food but also one of the favourite butts of their humour! (The service was, however, reintroduced just six weeks later.) The travelling public were also asked to restrict the amount of luggage they carried, and for a time a ban was placed on the taking of any flowers on to trains!

Tom Walters, a former railwayman who lives in Derby, recalled an amusing incident that happened on 3 September at his local station. 'One of the station porters found a package that was ticking in the luggage van of a train that stopped at Derby. He was convinced it must be a bomb and quickly dropped it into a bucket of water. When the ticking stopped, the package was opened very gingerly. Inside was found a waterlogged clock, some jewellery, several hundred pounds in

A railway poster urging passengers to think twice before travelling on the overcrowded lines.

THE RAILWAY EXPERT

Returning from rehearsal evacuation in a Northern town, a small girl of between ten and twelve sat down next to me in the train. 'Looks like we're on track for a war', she remarked.

'It rather does,' I said.

'Looks like Hitler's been up to some nasty underhand tricks – in with Russia and all.'

'You seem to know a lot about it,' I said.

'Aye, I do. But my brother knows more. He reads all the papers and knows all about them foreign countries and what they're up to. You should hear him talk to me Mother about it. Argue, argue, argue all day long.'

'How old is your brother?' I asked casually, imagining a young man rising military age.

'Oh,' she said, 'turned seven.'

From 'Four Winds' column in *Time & Tide*, 2 September 1939

Early in the year, the names of railway stations were obliterated in case the enemy invaded.

The London Underground system proved an ideal 'dormitory' for the capital's citizens when air raids were threatened.

notes and two bank books all apparently belonging to a woman who was travelling from Scotland to Staffordshire!'

In London, the famous Underground system proved not only one of the safest and most efficient means of getting to and from their jobs for the capital's workers, but when the air raids came later, it proved an ideal refuge for all those living in the city. Indeed, while large numbers of Londoners slept peacefully on the platforms, late-night and early-morning workers stepped carefully over them to board their trains.

The Underground was also a blaze of colour in contrast to the gloomy world above, for while the city was shrouded in darkness because of the blackout, the subterranean stations blazed with light, cheering all who had to use them. The Underground, in fact, provided many happy memories for those who had to stay in London throughout the war. One of the clearest of these memories concerns the cartoon character 'Billy Brown of London Town' a dapper little man in a pin-stripe suit and bowler hat created for the London Transport Authority by the *Daily Mirror* cartoonist David Langdon, and featured in countless thousand posters throughout the system. His purpose was to keep travellers informed about all aspects of the service as well as urging them to be public-spirited in the face of all the restrictions. A typical Billy Brown cartoon and verse appear on these pages.

A typical British family listening to their radio as war is declared. Note the gas masks at the ready!

10 Keep in Touch with the Wireless

It was the radio – or 'wireless' as it was then generally called – which first brought the news of the declaration of war to the men, women and children of Britain, and from the moment of the Prime Minister's announcement on that Sunday morning, the service enjoyed a five-year period of unprecedented importance in everyday life by providing the first and most important single source of news and information. Although it is true to say that not every home in the country possessed one of these rather crude-looking sets which resembled wooden boxes with a simple tuning dial and on–off switch, there were well in excess of 8,500,000 licence holders in September 1939.

Even before war had been sombrely declared by Neville Chamberlain in what will forever be remembered as his most effective speech – perhaps one of *the* most effective radio speeches of all time – the BBC had prepared itself for war by breaking up its network of eight regional stations and concentrating all its energies and resources into a single programme, the Home Service, broadcast on 391 metres (Northern) and 449 (Scottish). In both broadcasting and government circles it had already been realized that this was going to be the first war in history when the power of radio would make it possible to announce all crucial events, victories and defeats, almost the moment after they had occurred. Therefore the influence of the wireless could be vital and far-ranging.

Explaining how the change-over had been made through a complicated set of technical engineering arrangements, the Director-General of the BBC, F. W. Ogilvie, said in a broadcast to the nation on 8 September: 'The various parts of our forces were mobilized, according to plan, for their work in different parts of the country. Within a couple of days a special number of *Radio Times* was put out with details of new programmes; and from the middle of the week, the amount of real, live material broadcast had begun to increase steadily. Of course, we had to plan to use a lot of gramophone records in the interval, but I'm sure you'll agree that three or four days was not an excessive allowance for carrying out this complete revolution in our system.

'What of the future? Our object is, and will be, to continue to give you the best possible service, whatever conditions may be; to continue to give you a news service which is truthful and objective; to give you talks, plays, variety, orchestras, dance music, feature

Richard Dimbleby, arguably the most famous broadcaster to emerge during the war years.

MONDAY September 4

767 kc/s 391.1 m. and 668 kc/s 449.1 m.

3.15   **LIGHT RECORDS**

3.30   **GRAMOPHONE RECORDS**

Webster Booth, Foster Richardson, and Dorothy Clarke
Benny Goodman and his Orchestra
Alfred Sittard (organ)
Tino Rossi (tenor)

4.0   **VARIETY**

on gramophone records

4.30   **TIME AND NEWS**

4.45   **SANDY MACPHERSON**

at the BBC Theatre Organ

Homage	*Haydn Wood*
Trees	*Rusbach*
I'll walk beside you	*Murray*
Wedding of the Painted Doll	*N. H. Brown*
Intermezzo (Cavalleria rusticana)	*Mascagni*
Hits of the Moment	*arr. Macpherson*

5.15   **GRAMOPHONE RECORDS**

The Louis Voss Grand Orchestra

Caledonia, a Scottish Fantasie in Modern Style............*Charrosin*

Maggie Teyte (soprano)

I'll follow my secret heart }
Nevermore   } ....*Coward*

The Leslie Bridgewater Harp Quintet

Down in the Forest.............................*Landon Ronald*
Prunella...................................*Bridgewater*

Derek Oldham (tenor)

Orchids to My Lady...............................*Carr*
Fleurette.....................................*McGeoch*

Frank Merrick (pianoforte)

Nocturne in A flat, No. 3.............. ....*Field*

Helen Guest (pianoforte)

Toccata in D.................................*D'Erlanger*

London Philharmonic Orchestra, conducted by John Barbirolli
A Children's Overture...............................*Quilter*

6.0   **Time Signal, Greenwich**

NEWS

6.15   **LONDON ANNOUNCEMENTS**
             SCOTTISH ANNOUNCEMENTS

6.25   **'FIRST STEPS IN FIRST AID'**

An easy course for everyone
By a doctor
1—General principles of first aid—bleeding and fractures—the
triangular bandage and its uses
See the diagrams on page 5

6.45   **LIGHT RECORDS**

7.0   **WELSH AND WESTERN ANNOUNCEMENTS**

7.15   **LIGHT RECORDS**

7.30   **Time Signal, Greenwich**

NEWS

7.45   **NORTHERN ANNOUNCEMENTS**

8.0   **VARIETY**

on gramophone records

8.30   **'SHIP ON TRIAL'**

A recorded impression of the trials of a modern liner
Produced by Victor Smythe

9.0   **Time Signal, Greenwich**

NEWS

9.15   **'TONIGHT'S TALK'**

A series of talks on important topics of the day

9.30   **VARIETY**

on gramophone records

10.0   **SANDY MACPHERSON**

at the BBC Theatre Organ

The Washington Post	*Sousa*
Minuet in G	*Beethoven*
Serenata	*Toselli*
Do you remember ?—A medley of popular hits from the first musical films	*arr. Andrews and Lewin*
A Kiss in the Dark	*Herbert*
Just like a melody from out of the sky	*Donaldson*
The Lost Chord	*Sullivan*

10.30   **Time Signal, Greenwich**

NEWS

10.45   **MIDLAND AND NORTHERN IRELAND**
              ANNOUNCEMENTS

11.0   **VARIETY**

on gramophone records

11.30   **THE BBC NORTHERN ORCHESTRA**

Overture, Fra Diavolo	*Auber*
Suite No. 1, L'Arlésienne	*Bizet*

Time Signal, Greenwich at 12.0

12.0 - 12.15   **NEWS**

The first day of war – and the Radio Times *lists just two 'live' shows, both by Sandy Macpherson at the BBC Theatre organ. Otherwise, broadcasting was a ceaseless flow of gramophone records – a point cleverly satirized by cartoonist J. W. Taylor.*

" *This is the B.B.C. Home Service. Ladies and Gentlemen—a gramophone record !* "

programmes – the best entertainment possible of all sorts. As in the past, the regular broadcasting of religious services will seek to bear witness to the things of the spirit. And we're not forgetting the children; it's their world also now, and it will be theirs later on to make better. "Children's Hour" has begun again already, and so have our schools broadcasts, which should prove to be even more valuable now, under the new conditions of evacuation.

'So much for the Home Service. For listeners overseas we are broadcasting continuously for twenty-two hours out of the twenty-four, right around the world. What listeners overseas are chiefly looking for is truthful and objective news; to meet that need as best we can, the output of our overseas news service since Friday last has been more than doubled.'

Just how speedily and efficiently the new Home Service put the D-G's plans into effect can be judged from columnist George Buchanan's report in *The Spectator* of 15 September:

'In the first days of the war the radio bulletins became a focal point in millions of homes. The essential difference between the function of the radio and the Press was demonstrated sharply, as never before. The radio can disseminate as no other instrument can; with the Press lies the role of recapitulation, amplification, interpretation and comment – all such after-thinking as follows the first eager grasping of information.

'Whereas Press news is imbibed singly, radio news is usually imbibed in groups. You can walk down a street and hear the same voice busy in every house. Thus radio news is community news: it is a united gesture of a society listening at the same time. We have a sense of undergoing the same situation together.'

Turning to the broadcasts themselves, Mr Buchanan added: 'So far the bulletins have been vigorously and well delivered with few exceptions – impersonal and without melodrama. Certain announcers, speaking without modulation or inflexion, achieve a mechanical fixated tone, but this deficit is preferable to any contrary defect. They tell us breezily of monstrous events, and this is better than breathy, over-impressed voices. It was as well, though, that the long weather forecast was dropped. At first it was as if, in answer to our question, "How's the war?" we were told, "They'll have a fine day for it."'

It was not long before the voices of some of these announcers became as familiar to listeners as members of their own family, and though it was not until May 1940 that they were able to give their names, news readers such as Bruce Belfrage, John Snagge, Alvar Lidell and Freddie Grisewood were soon instantly identifiable to the vast army of listeners grouped silently around their sets for the bulletins which began at 7 a.m. and continued, mostly on the hour with those at 6 p.m. and 9 p.m. considered the most important, until midnight. Later, the ranks of these 'celebrities' were to be swelled by the great war correspondents such as Richard Dimbleby, Wynford Vaughan Thomas and Frank Gillard, all of whom seemed to be forever in the thick of the action. Long after the war was over, the names of these men were to remain firmly fixed in the consciousness of a deeply grateful nation.

Radio also made the reputations of a number of variety artists and comedians whose programmes were to become required listening for the war-weary seeking a little light relief. The first of these was a weekly show called *Garrison Theatre*, broadcast from Clifton Parish Hall in Bristol, where the BBC Variety Department had been evacuated. The star of the show was a versatile artist named Jack Warner who later became the lead in one of television's most favourite series, *Dixon of Dock Green*.

A SONG FOR TODAY?

The BBC should assist in inducing people in civil life to carry on as they usually do. Somebody asked me today what the soldiers would sing in this war. I haven't the faintest idea. But I think that no bad song for the BBC could be made out of an adaptation of one from the last war. Only three verbal alterations have to be made and you get:

'Pack up your Goebbels in your old kit-bag,
And Heil! Heil! Heil!'
And:
'What's the use of Goering?'

P.S.   I suppose the string of records on the radio at the moment may be due to technical difficulties, but a few persons in person – e.g. Miss Gracie Fields – would be welcomed!

J. C. Squire, editor of *Punch*, 5 September 1939

Jack, who was born Horace John Waters in London in October 1896, changed his stage name to avoid comparison with his two famous older sisters who were also entertainers, Elsie and Doris Waters. It is also a not generally appreciated fact that Jack was one of the first stars of television.

'Back in the thirties I formed this partnership with Jeff Darnell doing comic songs and impressions,' Jack explained in an interview in 1971. 'We broadcast on radio many times and then in 1936 made the first of many appearances on television. They were very early days and there were only about 500 sets in London. We were on with a ballet show once and another time with an American conjuror. The make-up was terrible and the heat awful!'

Jack was in fact out of work and out of money when war was declared, but realizing the BBC would need entertainers, quickly offered his services to the Variety Department in Bristol. Plans were already being made for *Garrison Theatre* which would supposedly be performed by men from the services in front of an audience of troops – and Jack seemed ideally suited to play a cheeky Cockney soldier.

It was a case of perfect timing, and within a matter of weeks the programme was the number one radio show. Jack actually wrote all his own material for *Garrison Theatre*, performed monologues such as 'Frank and his Tank' and sang songs like 'A Funny Occupation' and 'I'm a Bunger-up of Rat-'oles'. He also read out letters from 'my Bruvver Sid', a serving soldier, which produced one of the earliest catch-phrases of the war – 'blue pencil!', signifying a place where the military censor had deleted something which the audience anticipated as a colourful adjective. This phrase soon became the national substitution for swearwords!

Jack was also responsible for another much-repeated catch-phrase, as he explained in 1971: 'Every week we used to try to work out a different way for me to come in. One time I'd come in from the wings, another time I'd come up through the orchestra. So one week I decided I'd ride down the stalls on a bike shouting as I came, "Mind my bike!" So I made this silly entrance for about four weeks and then we decided to do something different, and we had about 3000 letters all asking, "Why have you stopped saying 'Mind my bike'?"

'But I did have one from a man who said: "Dear Sir, I like your programme very much, but I've spent hundreds of pounds on my boy's education and the only thing he says is 'Mind my bike!'" Everybody was talking about *Garrison Theatre*, you see. It came along at a psychological time when everybody was feeling a bit miserable. And for me it was a heaven-sent thing. I was up in the golden bracket in about three weeks!'

Another radio show which had actually started on 12 July was also to earn a special place in the heart of the nation: *It's That Man Again*, better known by the initials *ITMA*, and starring Tommy Handley. The title had originally been selected as a reference to Hitler, but when the show was relaunched by the Home Service on 19 September it now more specifically referred to Handley as the 'Minister of Aggravation and Mysteries at the office of Twerps'. *ITMA* became a triumphant mixture of nonsense, absurdity, topical

Jack Warner's 'blue-pencil letters' became a catch-phrase and made him a radio star right at the start of the war.

TWO BLUE-PENCIL LETTERS
BY Jack Warner

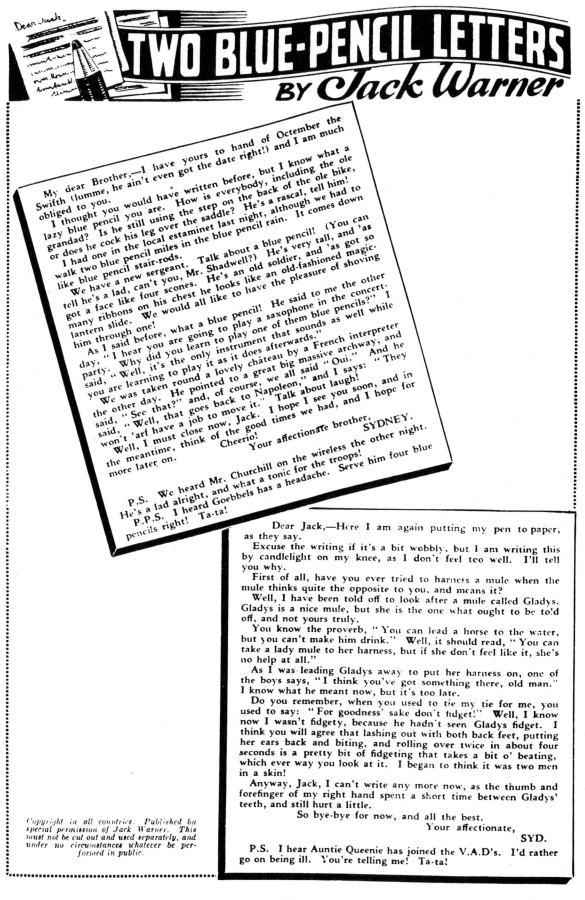

My dear Brother,—I have yours to hand of Octember the Swifth (lumme, he ain't even got the date right!) and I am much obliged to you.

I thought you would have written before, but I know what a lazy blue pencil you are. How is everybody, including the ole grandad? Is he still using the step on the back of the ole bike, or does he cock his leg over the saddle? He's a rascal, tell him!

I had one in the local estaminet last night, although we had to walk two blue pencil miles in the blue pencil rain. It comes down like blue pencil stair-rods.

We have a new sergeant. Talk about a blue pencil! (You can tell he's a lad, can't you, Mr. Shadwell?) He's very tall, and 'as got a face like four scones. He's an old soldier, and 'as got so many ribbons on his chest he looks like an old-fashioned magic-lantern slide. We would all like to have the pleasure of shoving him through one!

As I said before, what a blue pencil! He said to me the other day, "I hear you are going to play a saxophone in the concert-party. Why did you learn to play one of them blue pencils?" I said, "Well, it's the only instrument that sounds as well while you are learning to play it as it does afterwards."

We was taken round a lovely château by a French interpreter the other day. He pointed to a great big massive archway, and said, "See that?" and, of course, we all said "Oui." And he said, "Well, that goes back to Napoleon," and I says: "They won't 'arf have a job to move it." Talk about laugh!

Well, I must close now, Jack. I hope I see you soon, and in the meantime, think of the good times we had, and I hope for more later on.

Cheerio!

Your affectionate brother,

SYDNEY.

P.S. We heard Mr. Churchill on the wireless the other night. He's a lad alright, and what a tonic for the troops!

P.P.S. I heard Goebbels has a headache. Serve him four blue pencils right! Ta-ta!

Dear Jack,—Here I am again putting my pen to paper, as they say.

Excuse the writing if it's a bit wobbly, but I am writing this by candlelight on my knee, as I don't feel too well. I'll tell you why.

First of all, have you ever tried to harness a mule when the mule thinks quite the opposite to you, and means it?

Well, I have been told off to look after a mule called Gladys. Gladys is a nice mule, but she is the one what ought to be told off, and not yours truly.

You know the proverb, "You can lead a horse to the water, but you can't make him drink." Well, it should read, "You can take a lady mule to her harness, but if she don't feel like it, she's no help at all."

As I was leading Gladys away to put her harness on, one of the boys says, "I think you've got something there, old man." I know what he meant now, but it's too late.

Do you remember, when you used to tie my tie for me, you used to say: "For goodness' sake don't fidget!" Well, I know now I wasn't fidgety, because he hadn't seen Gladys fidget. I think you will agree that lashing out with both back feet, putting her ears back and biting, and rolling over twice in about four seconds is a pretty bit of fidgeting that takes a bit o' beating, which ever way you look at it. I began to think it was two men in a skin!

Anyway, Jack, I can't write any more now, as the thumb and forefinger of my right hand spent a short time between Gladys' teeth, and still hurt a little.

So bye-bye for now, and all the best.

Your affectionate,

SYD.

P.S. I hear Auntie Queenie has joined the V.A.D's. I'd rather go on being ill. You're telling me! Ta-ta!

The great Tommy Handley (centre), *star of the most famous wartime radio show,* ITMA, *with his scriptwriter Ted Kavanagh* (right) *and musical director Charles Shadwell. The three men are discussing a future script during a stint of fire-watching in September 1939.*

satire, word play, catch-phrases and some of the most unusual characters ever created.

Tommy Handley was a Liverpool-born comic who had made his debut on radio in 1925. Following the success of *ITMA* he was said to be the most highly paid regular entertainer on the BBC, averaging about £320 per week, although it has been estimated that the show

called Fusspot and a German spy Funf, along with Dorothy Summers as an indomitable charlady, Mrs Mopp. Among the many catch-phrases this trio gave to the nation were, 'I don't mind if I do', 'Can I do you now, sir?', 'After you, Claude – No, after you Cecil' and 'TTFN' – 'Ta Ta For Now'.

Paying tribute to Tommy Handley after his death in 1949, Eric Maschwitz, a former Variety Director of the BBC, said: 'Tommy, together with his scriptwriter Ted Kavanagh and producer Francis Worsley, created more lovable characters than even Walt Disney. Like Disney's enchanting animals, they had a clear-cut comical simplicity that appealed to children of all ages in Buckingham Palace and pre-fab alike. There has never been a comic entertainment by microphone to equal the *ITMA* series.' Not without good reason has *ITMA* since been referred to as 'probably the finest morale-raiser of the war'.

Also relaunched at the same time as *ITMA* was the Saturday night show *Band Waggon*, which starred the diminutive comedian 'Big-Hearted' Arthur Askey, Richard 'Stinker' Murdoch, Syd Walker and Charles Smart. In announcing the return of the show, Askey, who also originated from Liverpool and had graduated from clerking to concert-party work followed by variety, radio and films, told his listeners, 'Hello, play-mates – I think it's a stroke of genius putting *Band Waggon* on the air. It'll make old Nasty realize what the British public will put up with. Anyway, they had to do something to give the gramophone a rest!'

Askey himself was responsible for introducing what became one of the most popular songs of the war, an adaptation of Noel Gay's pre-war tune 'Run, Rabbit, Run' which the little comic sang as 'Run, Adolf, Run'. After appearing with Askey, Murdoch was to go on to further fame in the series *Much Binding in the Marsh* about the most notorious RAF station in the country, in which he co-starred with Kenneth Horne. Curiously, despite all his popularity, Arthur Askey was never given a wartime show of his own.

Another entertainer for whom the war made a new reputation was Robb Wilton, who originated the famous catch-phrase which is also the title of this book, 'The Day War Broke Out'. Yet another comic to have been born in Liverpool (in 1881 as plain Robert Smith), Robb gave up a career in engineering to become a serious actor before discovering his true talent in burlesquing characters like policemen, firemen, magistrates and others.

Robb was already well known to listeners in 1939 for playing Mr Muddlecombe, JP, a bewildered and rather solemn official trying to combine dignity with inaction. One of the sketches featuring this character had not long beforehand earned a protest to the BBC from the

itself cost less than £1000 per week to produce.

What made *ITMA* so memorable was the fun it had at the expense of wartime restrictions and bureaucracy. Complementing Handley's virtuoso performances as the Minister – and later the Mayor of Foaming-at-the-Mouth – were Jack Train as the blustering and boozing Colonel Chinstrap, a civil servant

Another big favourite of the war years was
'Big-Hearted' Arthur Askey, the star of Band Waggon.

The ROMANCE of BAND WAGGON

*Photo:
Mannell,
London*

KENNETH BLAIN

SYD WALKER

"BIG - HEARTED"
ARTHUR

HARRY S. ('BISHOP')
PEPPER

RICHARD ('STINKER')
MURDOCH

GORDON CRIER

Magistrates Association. Objection was made to Robb's performance as a magistrate conducting a case under the influence of drink and asking a pretty female witness to meet him in a public house after the trial was over. The BBC pointed out that the broadcast was so farcical and the charges – such as racing tortoises within the 30-mile limit – so obviously fantastic, that it was not felt that it could be regarded as any reflection on magistrates' courts. Robb himself expressed surprise at the complaint, recalling that the best audience he had ever had for a send-up of the police force had been a group of policemen!

What made Robb Wilton still more popular were the monologues he began in September 1939, playing a patriotic but hen-pecked citizen anxious to support the war effort but constantly frustrated by his own stupidity and his wife's lack of co-operation. 'The day war broke out,' he would invariably begin these stories, 'my wife said to me . . .' and then launch into a tale of how he had failed as a special constable, or as a fire watcher, or, most famous of all, as a Home Guard.

For many people who spent the war at home, Robb Wilton was without doubt the outstanding comedian of the day, and his melancholy voice was widely imitated – especially in repeating his unforgettable catch-phrase. He was unforgettable, too, for lines such as Mr Muddlecombe's, 'We have many grave responsibilities, but at the moment I cannot think of any!'; and perhaps even more so for the following exchange with his wife on his becoming a new Home Guard officer.

'I'm supposed to stop Hitler's army landing,' Robb explained.

'What *you?*' came the disparaging reply, 'I think we'd stand a better chance if you were on the other side!'

But perhaps the man who (though unknowingly) gave British radio listeners their best laughs during the war actually *was* on the other side: William Joyce, 'Lord Haw-Haw' as he was nicknamed, the former Fascist, attempting to convince his audience to give up their fight against Germany. Though many considered him foolish, others felt that he had a sinister influence on some listeners because not a few of his predictions proved uncannily correct. It was equally true that many statements attributed to him were actually the product of local gossip and fertile imaginations. For comedians,

British listeners were warned against listening to foreign broadcasts – especially those of 'Lord Haw-Haw', William Joyce (opposite), the fascist traitor who was on the radio daily from Germany.

What do I do...

if I come across German or Italian broadcasts when tuning my wireless?

I say to myself: " Now this blighter wants me to listen to him. Am I going to do what he wants?". I remember that German lies over the air are like parachute troops dropping on Britain — they are all part of the plan to get us down — *which they won't*. I remember nobody can trust a word the Haw-Haws say. So, just to make them waste their time, I switch 'em off or tune 'em out !

Cut this out—and keep it !

Issued by the Ministry of Information

Space presented to the Nation by The Brewers' Society

The immortal 'Uncle Mac', Derek McCulloch, the favourite of every young listener during the war – including the author!

though, his indeterminate accent (he was Anglo-Irish, but had been born in America) and his opening line 'Jairmany calling' were a godsend, while newspaper and magazine cartoonists found him an endless source of jokes.

The daily broadcasts of 'Lord Haw-Haw' were not the only thing listeners found to complain about. One of the first productions of the BBC's drama department, an adaptation of Mrs Henry Wood's classic, *East Lynne*, was thought to be unsuitable because of its tragic story, while a retelling of the events of 'The Murder in the Red Barn' when a lecherous squire, William Corder, murdered his pregnant girlfriend, was condemned as unsuitable because 'there is too much mass murder going on in the world without these artificial aids to gloom'.

Such objections were few and far between, however, and BBC radio undoubtedly did much to keep British spirits high in those September days – and in the months and years that followed. In February 1940 a second network, the Forces Programme, opened to provide background listening and entertainment. Three months later another wartime favourite made its debut, *The Kitchen Front*, which featured the cheery talks of the 'Radio Doctor', Charles Hill, later to become the Postmaster General and Chairman of the BBC. His exhortations to listeners to open their bowels every day in order to ensure good health became almost as famous as many of the comedians' catchphrases! January 1941 also saw the arrival of *Any Questions?* which soon changed its name to *The Brains Trust* and with a panel consisting of a philosopher, Professor Joad, a scientist, Professor Julian Huxley, and a retired naval officer, Commander Campbell, became the first serious programme ever to attract a mass audience of the size of those for *Garrison Theatre* and *ITMA*. The Forces Programme also introduced the long-running series *Workers' Playtime*, in which top artists broadcast live from factories during the lunch breaks.

No discussion of wartime favourites would be complete without mention of Sandy Macpherson, the theatre organist who was summoned back from holiday to open the Home Service programmes on 2 September and was rarely off the air-waves for the rest of the war – despite losing his organ in an air raid in 1940! For much of this time he was host of his own show, *Sandy's Half Hour*, which in some weeks attracted over 5000 requests for tunes.

For younger listeners, after a four-day break 'Children's Hour' returned on 6 September, with 'Uncle Mac', the consummately professional broadcaster, Derek McCulloch, at the helm. Many of the programmes in the early days depended on his resourcefulness

---

HAVE YOU FORGOTTEN THE LAST WAR?

German people – have you forgotten what you and others suffered in the last war? We have not forgotten, and that is why Mr Chamberlain has waited and has made concessions until today. But we could not rely on the promises of your Fuehrer.

Remember Mr Chamberlain's flight to Munich a year ago? It was the moment when Germany wanted to make war on Czechoslovakia. Do you remember what Hitler said shortly before he took the Czech frontier fortifications? 'We don't want any Czechs,' said Hitler – and six months later he invaded Czechoslovakia.

Do you remember what Hitler said in 1937? 'I don't intend to attack Austria' – and a year later he marched into Vienna and the name of Austria was eliminated from the map.

In 1935 Hitler, speaking of the non-aggression pact with Poland, concluded in 1934, promised not to attack Poland and to keep his word. Now your army attacks Poland and your newspapers tell atrocity tales about Poland identical to those told a year ago about Czechoslovakia.

Do you remember the time when he spoke about the doctrine of Bolshevism and expressed a determination that his own people should never be contaminated by it and that he would under no circumstances ask for help from Russia? And now your worst enemy of yesterday has become your best friend of today.

Why another war? Because your government wants to dominate the world by force, heedless of liberty and heedless of pledges!

BBC broadcast to Germany, 3 September 1939

---

at filling in through lack of material or unsuitable scripts, though there were always weekly highlights like the stories of 'Toytown' and the talks on country life given by 'Romany'. But for anyone who was a child at the time and listened to 'Children's Hour' during the war years, one memory undoubtedly surpasses all others. As a little boy myself growing up through those dark days, the voice of 'Uncle Mac' was warmly reassuring no matter what threats there might be of bombings or warnings of the possibility of invasion. And just like millions of others, I went happily to bed with his closing words ringing gently in my ears: 'Good night children, *everywhere*.'

11 When the TV Screens went Blank

It is perhaps surprising to discover that in the autumn of 1939, Britain possessed not only the first but also the best regular television service in the world. Despite the fact that the viewing range did not stretch much beyond London into the eastern counties and that there were only approximately 25,000 viewers with sets, the BBC Television Service was still well ahead of that in America which would not open with sponsored programmes until 1941. All of which makes the dramatic closing-down of the service on 1 September without a word of warning and very little explanation afterwards all the more strange.

The BBC had begun transmitting what was the world's first television service from their station at Alexandra Palace in north London on 2 November 1936. Less than two years later the number of viewers was well into five figures and there were sixteen different firms manufacturing TV sets with 12-inch screens which could be purchased for around £40 each. (There were even efficient small sets on sale for as little as £22!)

The quality of reception of the black and white pictures had also improved dramatically over these years, and what had at first been seen as a 'miraculous medium' was on the way to becoming the staple fixture in every home that it has now become. Without the interruption of the war – and the service's closure until 1946 – it might well have achieved this objective considerably sooner.

By September 1939, BBC TV had shown itself proficient at televising sport, offering viewers the Boat Race, the FA Cup Final, a number of professional boxing matches and, in August 1938, coverage of the England *v* Australia Test match from The Oval.

Everything transmitted by the medium went out 'live' which, though this inevitably produced the occasional hitch and even moments of unintentional humour, did not deter the BBC from launching into televising drama and features. J. B. Priestley's play 'When We Are Married' was a notable triumph in November 1938, as was 'The Parnell Commission', the first feature, and 'Tristan and Isolde', the first opera. Among the well-known actors to appear before the cameras in these pioneer days of TV were Laurence Olivier, Ralph Richardson and Cicely Courtneidge. Variety shows had also proved popular with viewers

and among the comedians who had come to the fore were Tommy Trinder, Douglas Byng, Lupino Lane and Tommy Handley, who, of course, became one of radio's biggest stars during the war.

Although over 60 per cent of viewers in June 1939 thought the TV programmes were 'satisfactory', according to *The Listener* Research Survey (only 6 per cent did not), and as many as 80 per cent thought they were getting better, a recently set up 'watchdog' body, the Television Development Sub-Committee, was not altogether happy. According to Professor Asa Briggs, the foremost historian of public broadcasting in Britain: 'Their tastes were undisguisedly lowbrow. They did not like "morbid, sordid and horrific plays"; they were sceptical about foreign cabaret and ballet; and they were unmoved by Handel's "Acis and Galatea". They objected to studio items being presented twice, a practice which was necessitated by the meagre programme allowance.'

What everyone, the viewers and the Television Development Sub-Committee, was in complete agreement about was that they preferred women announcers to men – a fact in complete contrast to sound radio audiences who were united in favour of men!

In the days immediately before the declaration of war, the television service endeavoured to continue as though nothing was happening, a point made interestingly by Grace Wyndham Goldie, the first television reviewer, in her weekly column in *The Listener*. Writing in the issue dated 31 August, she said: 'Last week's programmes were a treat. I might almost call them a fair treat. For they were designed for the crowd, dominated by the needs of Radiolympia (the annual exhibition of broadcasting held in London). Did we want to see what television can do with singing? Here was Paul Robeson. With ballet? We were shown Alice Markova. Outdoor stuff? There was test match cricket and there were tours of the Zoo. Funny men? Here was Naunton Wayne at the top of his form; here were the Kentucky Minstrels; and here were two clowns, Bood and Bood, who were new to me and entirely first rate.'

The only criticism Miss Wyndham Goldie could find was one common to all these presentations. 'As soon as there are more than two people on the television screen,' she said, 'and most ballet and most comedy require more than two people, the difficulty of showing any relation between them either for aesthetic or comic effect is very evident. Let them be seen simultaneously and they become small, distant and ineffective; let them be seen in successive camera shots and the interplay between them becomes too heavily pointed, too clumsy and too slow. The easiest way out is to present one artist only and to see that that artist is so superlatively gifted that we are completely satisfied and want

Tommy Trinder, one of the first comedians to become a household name on the embryonic BBC Television Service.

no one else. This is what happened last week with both Miss Markova and Mr Wayne. So here again a major television difficulty was concealed by skilful choice of material.'

A week later, in the issue of 7 September, Miss Wyndham Goldie was again complimentary as well as being objective in the light of what had just happened in the world at large.

'Should the motto of entertainment in time of crisis be business as usual?' she aked her readers. 'Or should entertainment be sacrificed to instruction and information which may be useful to its audiences? This, obviously, is a decision which is not forced upon the theatre. But it is forced upon broadcasting and it was certainly forced upon television last week.

'The programmes were arranged. Should they be altered to give ARP demonstrations, short courses in first aid, instructions in fire-fighting, ways of dealing with sandbags, the handling of incendiary bombs and the like? The question is by no means simple. For the need for a rest from anxiety and for diversion for those who have the leisure to "look in" is probably at least as pressing as the need for instruction. And whatever the arguments, the television authorities in fact decided to give us the programmes virtually unaltered.'

This adherence to the schedule made what then happened on 'Black Friday' – as viewers were to refer to 1 September – all the stranger. For after another morning of transmissions from Radiolympia, a Mickey Mouse cartoon was screened and then at exactly midday, the plug was pulled: screens everywhere went blank. In the studios at Alexandra Palace, a drama production was also stopped in mid-rehearsal. The play was an adaptation of W. Somerset Maugham's 'The Circle' starring Alan Wheatley, Griselda Hervey, Belle Chrystall and a young man named James Mason. This prestigious and costly performance, for which lavish sets had already been built, was being produced by the head of television drama, Val Gielgud, and was set for live transmission on Sunday – the day war broke out.

Though many mystified viewers continued to try to adjust their sets for the scheduled afternoon programmes of a visit to London Zoo, Mantovani and his orchestra, and a variety show, their screens remained dark. In fact, the very last words heard on British TV

A family gathered around their tiny TV screen in 1939 in a room carefully curtained against the light.

RADIO TIMES, ISSUE DATED SEPTEMBER 1, 1939

September 3-9 TELEVISION

Transmission by the Marconi-EMI system. Vision, 45 Mc/s. Sound, 41.5 Mc/s. All timings on these pages are approximate.

From 11.0 a.m. to 12.0 noon each weekday films are shown for radio trade purposes only.

Should the television programme extend beyond 11.0 p.m. a recorded news bulletin will be given at the end of the programme, except on Sundays.

Sunday

7.55 National Programme (sound only)

8.5-10.20 'THE CIRCLE'
by W. Somerset Maugham
Cast
Arnold Champion-Cheney, M.P.
Alan Wheatley
Footman......................Henry Hallatt
Mrs. Shenstone........Griselda Hervey
Elizabeth....................Belle Chrystall
Edward Luton.............James Mason
Clive Champion-Cheney
Ronald Simpson
Lady Catherine................Eva Moore
Lord Porteous.............Aubrey Dexter

Production by Val Gielgud

To be repeated on September 11

Monday

3.0-4.15 Leon M. Lion
in
'A CUP OF HAPPINESS'
A Devonshire comedy by
Eden Phillpotts
Cast
Mrs. Bessie Veryard of Willowbrook
Farm......................Amy Veness
Adam Veryard, her elder son
Roger Livesey

Tom Veryard, her younger son
Lewis Stringer
Rose Veryard, her daughter
Janet Johnson
(by permission of Messrs. Payne-Jennings and Killick)
Tobias Gigg, her head man
Leon M. Lion
Milly Venn, her dairymaid
Winifred Hindle
(by permission of Gilbert Miller and Jack Buchanan)
Tod Bartlett, her huckster
John Boxer
Willie Yaw, a wise woman
Margaret Nicholls
Jonathan Berry, late huntsman of the
East Devon Foxhounds
Gilbert Davis
Jemima Didham, dairymaid at Hedge
Barton Farm.........Kay Bannerman

The action takes place during high summer on Willowbrook Farm at High Holberton, Devon

Settings designed by Barry Learoyd

Production by Michael Barry

★ ★ ★

8.0 National Programme (sound only)

9.0 BEATRICE LILLIE
At the piano, Sam Walsh

9.10 SPEAKING PERSONALLY
Dr. Edvard Beneš

9.20 NEWS FILM
British Movietonews

9.30 Seymour Hicks
in
'WAITING FOR A LADY'

'DOWN ON THE FARM'. The television camera will go down to Bulls Cross Farm on Wednesday, when A. G. Street and the farmer will talk over the month's work. Above you see Street with Jasmine Bligh surveying a Red Poll bull at Bulls Cross.

GRISELDA HERVEY and BELLE CHRYSTALL
play leading parts on Sunday in *The Circle*, thought by many to be Somerset Maugham's finest play.

9.50 'NANCY'S PUPPETS'
Presented by Nancy Worsfold and Elspeth Holland, accompanied on the recorder by Marjorie Gabain
in
'Pyramus and Thisbe'
from 'A Midsummer-Night's Dream'

10.5 CARTOON FILM
'The Grasshopper and the Ants'

10.10-10.20 PICTURE STORIES
'Love in Tonga'
and
'The Seventh Man'
two picture stories by Robert Gibbings

Tuesday

3.0-4.45 'THE PELICAN'
A drama by F. Tennyson Jesse and H. M. Harwood
Cast
General Sir John Heriot, Bart.
Athole Stewart
Lady Heriot........Mabel Terry Lewis
Hermione Blundell......Joyce Kennedy
Beadon, the butler....Stafford Hilliard
Marcus Heriot..............James Raglan
Charles Cheriton...........Eric Portman
Wanda Heriot, Marcus's wife
Mary Hinton
Anna, Wanda's servant
Agnes Lauchlan
Paul Lauzun................Austin Trevor
Robin......................Derek Elphinstone
Shaw, Sir John's valet
Arthur Goullet
Production by Lanham Titchener

★ ★ ★

8.0 Regional Programme (sound only)

8.47 app.   Interval

9.0   NEWS FILM
Gaumont-British News

9.10-10.25 'KNOCK, OR THE
TRIUMPH OF MEDICINE'
A comedy by Jules Romains, translated into English by Harley Granville Barker
Cast
Doctor Knock............Marius Goring
Doctor Parpalaid.......Morris Harvey
Mme. Parpalaid..........Marjorie Bryce
M. Bernard, a schoolmaster
J. Sebastian Smith
M. Mousquet, a chemist
Lawrence Hanray
A farmer's wife..............Amy Veness
Mme. Pons, a rich widow
Helen Haye
Mme. Remy............Elizabeth Maude
Scipio, a servant.........Stuart Latham
A nurse......................Freda Bamford
Two countrymen { Archie Harradine
                { Hugh Griffith

The action takes place in a small French country town at the present day

The settings designed by
Barry Learoyd

Adapted for television and produced by Eric Crozier

To be repeated on September 15

Wednesday

3.0 DOWN ON THE FARM
'September'
A. G. Street visits Bulls Cross Farm and surveys with the farmer the work to be done during the month of September

3.20 CABARET INTERLUDE
with
Mansfield and Lamar (dancers)
Zeanit (illusionist)
Trudi Binar (songs)

3.35   NEWS FILM
Gaumont-British News

PROGRAMMES

The Scanner's Television
News is on Page 15

3.45 'STYLE AT HOME'
Bettie Cameron Smail will explain and illustrate how to achieve the professional touch in home dressmaking
Presentation by Andrew Miller Jones

★ ★ ★

8.0 National Programme (sound only)

9.0 NEWS MAP
No. 1 (New Series)
Topical problems will be discussed by John Gunther, author of 'Inside Europe' and illustrated by J. F. Horrabin's maps
Presentation by Mary Adams

9.25 NEWS FILM
British Movietonews

9.35 MARIA ANTONIA DE CASTRO
Brazilian pianist

9.45 CARTOON FILM
'The Fox Hunt'

9.50 'STYLE AT HOME'
(Details as 3.45)

10.5-10.25 'THE CONDUCTOR SPEAKS—'
Eugene Goossens
The BBC Television Orchestra
Leader, Boris Pecker
Conducted by Eugene Goossens who will also speak on conducting
Presentation by Philip Bate

Thursday

3.0 CABARET
with
Chiezel (juggler)
Dela Lipinskaya (diseuse)
A. C. Astor (ventriloquist)

MR. MIDDLETON GETS DOWN TO IT. He will be at the Alexandra Palace garden on Saturday afternoon.

3.25 'THIS MOTORING'
illustrated in verse and cartoon by Reginald Arkell and Harry Rutherford

3.35 NEWS FILM
British Movietonews

3.45-4.0 'PICTURE PAGE'
(263rd edition)
A topical magazine
Edited by Cecil Madden
Produced by Val Gielgud
Interviewer: Leslie Mitchell
with Joan Miller

★ ★ ★

8.0 Regional Programme (sound only)

8.53 app. Interval

9.0 KEN JOHNSON AND HIS WEST INDIAN DANCE ORCHESTRA
with
Elisabeth Welch

9.30 NEWS FILM
Gaumont-British News

9.40-10.20 'PICTURE PAGE'
(264th edition)
(Details as 3.45)

Friday

3.0-4.25 'THE RISING SUN'
A play adapted from the Dutch of Heijermans by Christopher St. John
Cast
Matthew Strong, a tradesman
Harcourt Williams
(by permission of the Daniel Mayer Company, Ltd.)
Anna, his wife............Deirdre Doyle
(by permission of Gilbert Miller and Jack Buchanan)
Sonia, his daughter..Josephine Wilson

Old Strong, his father
Lawrence Hanray
Dorothy Mertens, a neighbour
Chris Castor
Nathaniel, her son, a schoolmaster
Wilfred Fletcher
Abraham, shop assistant at Strong's
Gerald Jerome
Christian Jensen, manager of 'The Rising Sun' Stores..Aubrey Dexter
Sand, a friend of Strong's
Warburton Gamble
The Deputy Attorney
Bernard Merefield
A police constable.....Rupert Siddons
An errand boy..........Edward Orchard
The action takes place in a little town in Holland and concerns the struggles of a small general shop against the new rival store—'The Rising Sun'
Production by Jan Bussell

★ ★ ★

8.0 National Programme (sound only)

9.0 BEBE DANIELS AND BEN LYON

9.15 BLOOD DONORS
A demonstration showing the simplicity with which the tests are made, how donors are classified into various groups, and the ease with which the minor operation of transfusion is carried out

9.35 NEWS FILM
British Movietonews

9.45 'CAPRICE'
An episode by Alfred de Musset, adapted and translated by Helen Simpson
Cast in order of appearance
Mathilde de Chavigny
Antoinette Cellier
A manservant..............Stuart Latham
Henri de Chavigny........Eric Portman
Madame de Lery....Cathleen Nesbitt
The scene is a boudoir in the Chavignys' house in Paris on a winter evening in the year 1837
Production by Royston Morley
To be repeated on September 12

10.10-10.40 Anton Dolin in 'SWANS'
A programme conceived by Poppœa Vanda, including an original Ballet for television
'The Swan of Tuonela'
Music by Sibelius
with
Wendy Toye
and
Keith Lester
The BBC Television Orchestra
Leader, Boris Pecker
Conductor, Hyam Greenbaum
Presentation by Philip Bate

Saturday

3.0 'IN OUR GARDEN'
C. H. Middleton in the Television Garden, Alexandra Park

DR. EDVARD BENES
will face the television camera for the first time on Monday.

3.15 CARTOON FILM
'Clock Store'

3.20 CARTOONS
by Oscar Berger

3.30 NEWS FILM
British Movietonews

3.40-4.5 AN IRVING BERLIN PROGRAMME
by
Eric Wild and his Band
with Diana Ward
and Gerry Fitzgerald
Presentation by Philip Bate

★ ★ ★

8.0 Regional Programme (sound only)

8.45 Interval

9.0 CABARET
with
Chiezel (juggler)
Dela Lipinskaya (diseuse)
A. C. Astor (ventriloquist)

9.30 NEWS FILM
Gaumont-British News

9.40 A demonstration of
BLACK AND WHITE BOXING
with Jack 'Dusty' Miller v. Company Sgt.-Major Wheeler, and a commentary by Major D. S. Lister

10.0 INTEREST FILM
'Free to Roam'

10.10 E. H. TATTERSALL
'This and That'

10.15-10.25 ALICE DE BELLEROCHE
(guitar)

Two behind-the-scenes photographs in the BBC studios at Alexandra Palace just before war broke out. (Below) A group of demurely dressed dancing girls performing on a variety show; and (opposite) the comedian Douglas Byng entertaining the cameraman – and his unseen audience – against a background of the most rudimentary scenery!

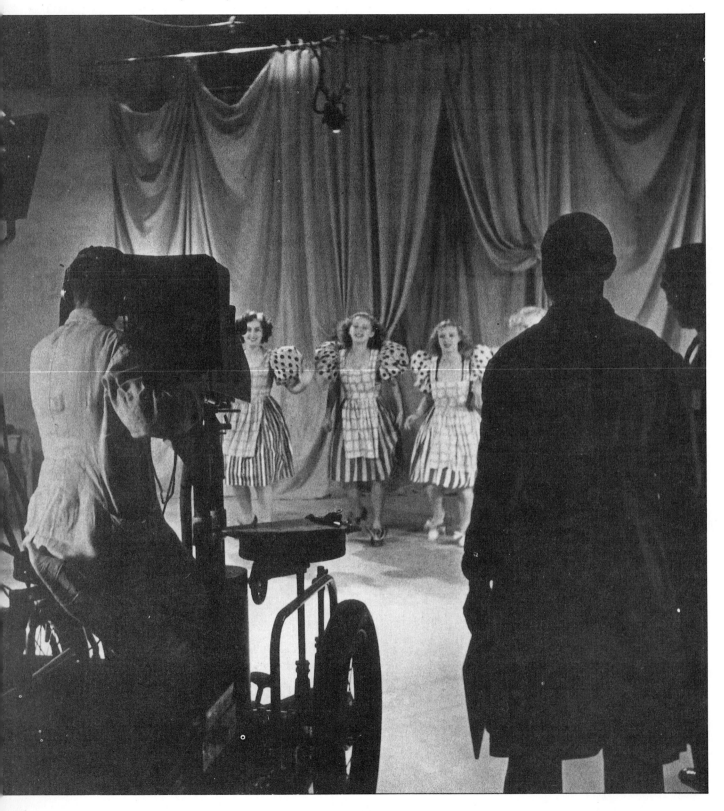

for what was to be almost seven years were those of Walt Disney's indefatigable mouse sighing resignedly, 'Ah tink ah go home.'

The BBC made no official announcement concerning the closure for several weeks, although *The Times* did carry this brief note on page 7 of its issue the next day: 'BBC Television service has been suspended until further notice.' When the Corporation did break its silence in the *Radio Times*, it showed a far from apologetic tone to the many thousands who had not only lost their pictures but suddenly found themselves with expensive and quite useless receivers in their living rooms. 'It has been pointed out to us,' the statement read, 'that nobody said a word in the *Radio Times* about the passing of television. That is quite

true, but so many things were passing, too, on that ominous weekend at the beginning of September, that television was at least not singled out for neglect. As a matter of fact we ourselves miss television as much as anyone.'

The official reason given for the closure was to free much-needed technicians for BBC Radio (television required ten men to radio's one). It was also hinted that a short-wave transmission such as television could help to guide enemy bombers to their targets, and the cost of operating the service in relation to its audience was very high. This, though, gave scant satisfaction to viewers who, it was estimated, had spent £750,000 on their sets, nor to the manufacturers who now had to scrap the 15,000 currently in production!

12 The Show Must Go On

For a large number of people the one cheering piece of news during the first weekend of September was the report that the singer Gracie Fields, the very epitome of happiness, was returning hurriedly to the country. A Reuter correspondent flashed this story to the nation's newspapers on 2 September:

'RETURN OF MISS GRACIE FIELDS: Miss Gracie Fields, looking much better than she did when she left England a month ago to travel to Capri, where she said she intended to have a six-month rest, returned yesterday. She said, "I am feeling very much better, but I shall not be working straight away. With the situation getting worse, I thought it was about time I returned home, for it's better to be with one's own folk under such conditions."'

To 'Our Gracie's' millions of fans in Britain this was heartening news indeed. For the Rochdale-born music-hall entertainer, who had risen to unprecedented fame in the early 1930s on the stage and in films as a singer and comedienne, somehow personified the British spirit of smiling through any adversity and her return, even though she was evidently far from completely well, brought a smile to every face. As an American entertainment writer, Ephraim Katz, was to comment some years later:

'The spirited, undaunted personality she portrayed helped spark optimism into the lives of British audiences. She was the top box-office draw and the highest-paid actress in Britain for most of the decade, and her popularity was so great that Parliament was once adjourned early so that members could go home to listen to one of her radio broadcasts.'

There seems little doubt that Gracie would have sustained this appeal unchallenged right through the war, but in 1940 she sadly had to leave the country for exile in America when her Italian-born husband, Monty Banks, was declared an alien by the British authorities following the entry of Mussolini's Italy into the war on the Axis side. Yet, even from Hollywood where she settled, Gracie still managed to send her messages of good cheer to Britain through records, films and radio broadcasts. Her award of Dame Commander of the British Empire given in 1979 was in no small measure due to her contribution to the war effort.

Like Gracie, a number of other entertainers were to play significant parts in keeping the nation smiling through the dark days, though show business itself had to recover from a blanket closure which was suddenly and to a degree unexpectedly imposed, 'until the scale of the German attack upon Britain is judged', by the Home Office on theatres, cinemas and dance halls immediately war was declared.

The reason for the closure was the Government's reasonable enough fear of the devastation that might be caused by the direct hit of a bomb on a crowded place of entertainment. The truth, though, was that the people as a whole felt more strongly about being deprived of their favourite singers, actors and film stars than some missile from Hitler's marauders. This was a view shared in all walks of life, and perhaps most powerfully stated by the author George Bernard Shaw in a letter to *The Times* of Tuesday 5 September.

'May I be allowed to protest vehemently,' the formidable writer began, 'against the order to close all theatres and picture houses during the war? It seems to me a masterstroke of unimaginative stupidity. During the last war we had 80,000 soldiers on leave to amuse every night. There were not enough theatres for them; and theatre rents rose to fabulous figures. Are there to be no theatres for them this time? We have hundreds of thousands of evacuated children to keep out of mischief and traffic dangers. Are there to be no pictures for them?

'The authorities, now all powerful, should at once set to work to provide new theatres and picture houses where these are lacking. All actors, variety artists, musicians and entertainers of all sorts should be exempted from every form of service except their own all-important professional one. What agent of Chancellor Hitler is it who has suggested that we should all cower in darkness and terror "for the duration"?'

Shaw's words were immediately supported by others, including many familiar voices from the worlds of the theatre and the cinema. Oswald Stoll, the theatre owner, for instance, argued for the re-opening of all places of entertainment as long as they observed blackout restrictions, and added tellingly that during the First World War 'no lives were lost in any theatres'.

Basil Dean, the former actor who had turned to film production and from 1932 headed Associated Pictures Ltd which first brought Gracie Fields to the screen, was even more vehement. 'Entertainment cannot be turned on and off like a tap,' Dean said, going on to explain the inevitable decline in standards of both film productions and stage presentations that would result from a prolonged closure. 'The authorities should seek the co-operation of the Entertainments National Service Association which is now in being,' he added.

A London showgirl at the Paradise Club prepares to entertain – appropriately wearing little more than a gas mask!

THIS IS A
NAAFI
SHOW

ORGANISED BY
ENSA

A typical Poster used by the ENSA touring groups in Britain.

Gracie Fields, 'Our Gracie', who raised the spirits of millions in Britain at the start of the war.

The arguments of these men and the general outcry from the public brought an about-turn from the Government and beginning in the week of 9 September, places of entertainment began to re-open their doors. In the meantime, though, some interesting developments had taken place. Not least of these was the immediate flourishing of Basil Dean's idea for the body of entertainers known as ENSA – letters which were later somewhat unkindly to be translated as 'Every Night Something Awful'! The first announcement of this new organization was made simply enough: 'British Equity,' a statement from the actors' union issued on 3 September declared, 'has been preparing for some time a register of actors over military age, who are unfit for active service, for work in a wartime theatre for entertainments for the Services and the civilian population. Actresses are also eligible for the register which is still open.'

In setting up the ENSA companies, Basil Dean made it quite clear that the organization should not be regarded as 'a giant foxhole' for actors and actresses wishing to avoid national service. By the second week of September, Dean had the first ENSA concert party performing for the troops, and before the year was out the organization was featuring many of the country's top stars including Gracie Fields, the actress Sybil Thorndike and comedian George Formby.

The chorus girls who appeared for ENSA were undoubtedly one of its greatest attractions among the servicemen and factory workers, though later, in 1942, there was very nearly a crisis when a proposal was made to call up all these girls between the ages of twenty-one and twenty-four! Fortunately, widespread protests from admirers caused the plan to be dropped. Also popular with the audiences were the ENSA comedians, though a number of them gained a reputation for telling risqué jokes and a handful were actually dismissed by Basil Dean, who proved himself a stern disciplinarian with his troupes by insisting that the men must wear evening dress and the women fashionable, though never flashy, costumes.

The dedication of these artists, though some undoubtedly had seen better days, did much for morale; and the performances, often given on makeshift stages or in small halls with poor acoustics, were more often than not a credit to performers who were earning only between £8 and £10 per week for much of the war!

When the lights went out in the London theatres on the night of Saturday 2 September there were some distinguished productions under way, though the tension of the past week had seen the size of audiences falling dramatically. At the famous Theatre Royal in Drury Lane, for example, where Ivor Novello was starring

A group of ENSA artists entertaining soldiers at an open-air concert in 1939; and (inset) an ENSA troupe 'on the road'!

with Mary Ellis in 'The Dancing Years', there were so few people in the gallery that Novello invited them to come forward and fill the empty seats in the stalls! (When 'The Dancing Years' did not re-open, Basil Dean actually took over Drury Lane for the headquarters of ENSA.)

At The Coliseum, Sarah Churchill was starring in 'Quiet Wedding', while a distinguished cast including John Gielgud, Edith Evans, Peggy Ashcroft, Jack Hawkins and Margaret Rutherford was appearing at The Globe in the Oscar Wilde classic 'The Importance of Being Earnest'. The popular husband-and-wife team of Jack Hulbert and Cicely Courtneidge were in 'the brilliant musical comedy show' 'Under Your Hat' at The Palace, while the inevitable Ben Travers farce, 'Spotted Dick' with Robertson Hare and Alfred Drayton, was still amusing audiences at The Strand.

The biggest stage success of the moment, though, was undoubtedly the Cockney musical 'Me and My Girl' which had recently completed 1000 performances at the Victoria Palace – the theatre having already become known by the title of its most popular tune, 'The home of "The Lambeth Walk"'. The stars were the irrepressible comic Lupino Lane and the vivacious Teddie St Dennis. Perhaps not surprisingly, 'Me and My Girl' was the first London show to re-open when the government restriction was relaxed (a couple of days ahead of an Agatha Christie mystery, 'Ten Little Niggers', which was to run right through the Blitz), and it seems somehow appropriate that, fifty years on from the day war broke out, the same musical, albeit revived, should still be playing to full houses in London's West End!

Swiftly re-opened, too, was the Windmill Theatre which remained as much a London institution throughout the war as it had been before. The nude girls who were the Windmill's great attraction continued to strip through all the trials of the war, and well earned the sobriquet 'We never closed' which the theatre boasted – and which some wags changed to 'We never clothed!'

At the London cinemas that weekend, the biggest box-office draw was a film topically billed as 'packed with British heroism', though it was actually American made (by Paramount) and starred only American actors including Gary Cooper, Ray Milland and Robert Preston. At least the author of the original book was British – Percival Christopher Wren. The film was the Foreign Legion classic *Beau Geste*. (A delightful misprint is to be found in *The Guardian* – then the *Manchester Guardian* – which notes: 'From today and all next week, *Beau Geste*, a new version of Police-constable Wren's romantic story of the French Foreign Legion'!)

Another popular film showing in London at the

INCORRECT WELSH – FROM NEATH!

The famous cartoonist H. M. Bateman was recruited for this poster campaign to warn about one of the dangers to be faced when visiting the cinema or theatre in wartime Britain!

The most popular show in London in September 1939 was 'Me and My Girl' with Lupino Lane in the leading role. Fifty years on, a new version of the show is again playing to packed houses in the capital.

Leicester Square Theatre was all about the great American President, *Young Mr Lincoln*, which starred Henry Fonda and had been directed by John Ford. (Ford's other classic, *Stagecoach*, was also showing in London at the Marble Arch Pavilion.) Across the square at the Odeon Theatre, the distinguished German actor Conrad Veidt (long resident in Hollywood) was starring in the topical espionage drama *The Spy in Black*, while Edward G. Robinson could be seen in *Confessions of a Nazi Spy* at The Regal, Marble Arch.

Two undeniably British stories that would earn classic status and which were also playing in the shadow of war were James Hilton's delightful story of a school-master, *Goodbye, Mr Chips* with Robert Donat and Greer Garson, at The Ritz, and the screen version of Daphne du Maurier's Cornish melodrama, *Jamaica Inn*, starring Charles Laughton and Maureen O'Hara, at The Rialto in Coventry Street. For those who wanted light relief, the indefatigable comedian Will Hay and his sidekicks, Graham Moffatt and Moore Marriott, could be seen in either *Oh! Mr Porter* at The Curzon or *Ask a Policeman* at The Stoll, while Clark Gable and Norma Shearer were on view in *Idiot's Delight* at several cinemas in London and the suburbs. An even greater escapist fantasy was playing at The Cameo, Charing Cross: the last episode of a Flash Gordon serial which was – the cinema said – 'to be followed next week by Larry (Buster) Crabbe in *Buck Rogers*, our new serial!'

There was also some slick opportunism about the provincial cinemas which, that Saturday night, were advertising the new Sally Ellers picture *They Made Her a Spy*. For on the billboards in brackets between the words 'a' and 'Spy' had been inserted the word 'NAZI'!

As a matter of record, on the day war broke out the Anna Neagle film about the First World War heroine Nurse Edith Cavell, directed by her husband Herbert Wilcox, opened in New York; while in Hollywood, Charlie Chaplin finally completed the script of what was to prove one of his most enduring masterpieces, the parody of Hitler entitled *The Great Dictator*. (Filming of the picture actually began on 9 September and was completed at the end of March 1940. The movie was premiered in London on 16 December 1940

The entertainer George Formby, who became a great favourite with the forces in films and special shows during the war.

at the height of the Blitz when Hitler seemed to many people a mere step away from imposing his dictator-ship on the nation: none the less, it was a huge success.)

It may seem curious in hindsight, but the first cinema to re-open after the emergency was far from the traditional cinema-going centres – it was, in fact, in the small Welsh coastal resort of Aberystwyth. Here the Pier Cinema opened its doors again on the afternoon of 5 September to show the western *Dodge City*, starring the actor later jokingly referred to as 'the man who won the war', Errol Flynn. This small piece of cinema history is recorded in the following anouncement to be found in the *Daily Mirror* of 6 September.

'The first cinema to re-open in the United Kingdom was in Aberystwyth yesterday. Permission for the opening was given by the Chief Constable of Cardiganshire, Captain J. J. Lloyd Williams, "subject to an operator being on duty during the whole of the performance to listen for air-raid warnings and sufficient staff to prevent panic in the event of any such warnings".'

Following Aberystwyth's lead – though the Home Office reproved the Chief Constable for jumping the gun – other cinemas re-opened their doors, and by 9 September cinema-goers were once again enjoying their favourite stars. Most showed very little apprehension about the possibility of a bomb bringing an end to their enjoyment of 'the pictures' and audiences were, if anything, bigger than before as people sought escape from the greyness of their wartime days. Cinemas could now also open for the first time on Sundays if they chose to cater for soldiers and war workers away from home.

Undoubtedly the most popular film of the war was *Gone With the Wind* released in 1939, though the most popular star was to prove the toothy George Formby from Wigan who had graduated from playing his ukelele in the northern music halls, to fame on the radio, and then to his greatest popularity in films such as *Trouble Brewing* (1939), *Let George Do It* (1940), and so on, one each year, throughout the war. His contribution in the form of songs with double meanings and lashings of slapstick comedy undoubtedly did much for his audiences' morale.

One of the best received individual pictures was *The First of the Few* (1942) starring Leslie Howard as the man who designed the Spitfire, and co-starring David Niven, the film star who left Hollywood on the outbreak of the war to join the army and was then 'recruited' to appear in this picture. Niven, who was actually a descendant of two generations of professional soldiers, later scored a personal triumph in *The Way Ahead* (1944) as an army officer trying to mould a group of new soldiers into a fighting unit.

The dance halls, which had similarly been forced to close on 3 September, were quickly back in business. Re-opening in the second week of September, they were soon more popular than ever, jam-packed with servicemen and girls anxious for any gaiety they could find. Initially the halls had to close at 10 p.m., but even when this was extended only until 11 p.m., nothing could dampen the enthusiasm.

The best-known dance band leaders of the time became even more in demand – musicians such as Billy Cotton, Geraldo, Henry Hall, Jack Jackson, Joe Loss, Mantovani, Jack Payne, Harry Roy and Victor Sylvester and their orchestras going through a period of unprecedented popularity. And when they weren't playing in public, the records of these bands seemed to be always on the radio.

There was also an immediate change in the kind of dances being requested, the quickstep rapidly outpacing all opposition, with the waltz and foxtrot following behind. Soon, there were even completely new wartime dances, the 'Blackout Stroll' devised by Tommy Connor being the first of these.

Talking about his reasons for creating this new dance, Tommy Connor said later, 'My main reason for getting the dance out was to get one which would allow a change of partner, and also bring an atmosphere of jollity on to the dance floors. There had been a seventy five per cent change of face in the ballrooms since the war began. Evacuees were going into ballrooms which they had never been in before. My dance gave them the party spirit. It made them happier and it gave everyone a reason to meet everyone else.'

The 'Blackout Stroll' was even claimed by its first publicity to be just what 'wallflowers' had long been seeking: 'You ladies called "wallflowers", fated to sit out all the dances, because perhaps your face isn't your fortune, or you aren't too good a dancer, or your figure isn't the cuddly kind, here's your chance to dance the "Blackout Stroll" – London's latest step is your Godsend!'

Another composer, Al Bollington, a BBC organist, came up with a song of the 'Blackout Walk', a variation of the 'Lambeth Walk' which ended with the words: 'Keep on smiling, don't be blue; don't let Hitler worry you!' At this time, too, a new dance version of the old Cockney tune 'Knees Up, Mother Brown' became a rage in many halls up and down the country.

David Niven, one of the most popular film stars in wartime Britain, in a scene from The First of the Few, *the story of the development of the Spitfire.*

Hard on the heels of all these dances was the first 'British Jitterbug Marathon' held at the Paramount Theatre, London, which received the following comment from the *News Chronicle*: 'Perhaps this noisy exhibition of abandoned convulsions was all in keeping with a mad world in which madmen are conflicting to dominate the continent!'

NAZIS JEER AT BRITISH SONG
No washing yet on Siegfried Line
Tommies are all in Paris

'We Are Hanging Out Our Washing on the Siegfried Line' was the subject of a contemptuous broadcast yesterday afternoon from Zeesen, the German short-wave station.

'We have made enquiries among German soldiers on leave from the Siegfried Line,' the speaker said. 'They report they have not seen a single Tommy between Luxembourg and the Palatinate frontier. But we hear from other sources that Tommies are arriving in great numbers – in Paris!

'Hotel-owners of the Montparnasse, managers of those queer little cafés that abound in Montmartre, and everybody in the Paris sight-seeing industry are hoping that the good old days when rich young Americans spent money like water have returned. And by Jove they are not far wrong.'

From the *Daily Telegraph*, 30 October 1939

Within ten days of the outbreak of war, the nation also had its first hit song, 'We're Gonna Hang Out the Washing on the Siegfried Line' by Jimmy Kennedy and Michael Carr, which soon inspired a host of other war tunes of varying quality. Among the most enduring from that autumn must surely be 'There'll Always be an England' by Ross Parker and Hughie Charles (which had sold 200,000 copies of sheet music by mid-November); the comedian Arthur Askey's adaptation of Noel ('Lambeth Walk') Gay's 'Run, Rabbit, Run' to 'Run, Adolf, Run', and Gracie Fields's very moving 'I'm Sending a Letter to Santa Claus, to Send Back My Daddy to Me'.

It was perhaps very apposite that the singer who had raised everyone's spirits by returning to her native country in September should have sung the song that brought some of the biggest smiles into that otherwise depressing first Christmas of the war.

ON THE ROAD WITH ENSA

Professional people in this war, I think, have been working just as hard, if not harder than the man behind the gun and 'the man behind the man behind the gun'. I don't think there has been a single artist who hasn't willingly and anxiously gone out and done everything he could against all sorts of odds.

Some of the difficulties – doing half a dozen shows a day with constant travelling in between – have been really trying, while others are amusing. One of the latter is getting your laundry done when you are constantly on the go, and I remember the scenes of boys in the orchestra washing their own clothes in hotel bathtubs and hanging them up to dry in their bedrooms – and wearing unironed shirts!

Basil Dean, the famed London producer, is in charge of ENSA and has done a wonderful job of organizing the shows. To many of the lesser known artists, these tours have proved a Godsend. Not only are they kept working, but those who are ineligible for the armed forces are thus made to feel that they are doing their bit. Then, too, a young crop of performers is being given a chance to develop. Some of these, with the continuous work, have already shown great promise.

I believe that we in the profession must consider it a privilege to know that we are putting in as many hours and as much effort as anyone else is to win this war. And I think that regardless of how desperate conditions are at times, folks get real pleasure out of the travelling troupes and it shows a definite need for entertainment to ease the strains of war.

Everywhere I travelled – in England, Scotland and Wales, and even Scapa Flow – I found audiences paying rapt attention to the shows. In many instances, the people refused to leave the theatres or factories even during air-raid warnings! During my short stay in London I was given proof not only by theatre owners, government officials and other performers, but observed myself, that England is definitely depending on the people of the theatre to keep morale at its highest pitch.

During my last tour in England, I generally gave three or four half-hour concerts a day, rising around 7 or 7.30 each morning and travelling 40 or 50 miles to the first factory. The factory concerts were usually given in the lunch hour – and with three shifts a day operating, lunch hour could be at practically any time! In many of these places, engines chugged away in the background providing real competition!

In the evenings, I usually sang in camps for the armed forces. I always put on a long dinner gown and tried to make myself as glamorous as possible to make these boys and girls in camps and factories feel that they were seeing a real, professional theatrical performance.

In England, I discovered that in every adversity there is always someone with a sense of humour. One of my favourite gags of the war is about Mr and Mrs Brown, who had heard the siren and were going down into the shelter. Mr Brown, being slightly ahead, shouted:

'Come on, Mary – 'urry up!'

'Wait a bit,' cried Mrs Brown. 'I can't find me teeth.'

To which Mr Brown replied: 'What do you think they're droppin' – sandwiches!'

Gracie Fields, writing in *Variety* after her arrival in America.

13 The Press Fights For Freedom

The newspapers, magazines and periodicals of Britain faced the outbreak of war with mixed emotions. Were they going to be able to continue? What restrictions might be placed on their editorial columns? And would their readers still have the inclination, not to mention the time, to read them? An article in *The Spectator* of 5 September accurately summarized the feelings in Fleet Street.

'War is generally supposed to be good for the daily papers, particularly the evening papers,' the commentary began, 'and this war may so far be running true to form. But unless conditions change considerably the papers will find life hard. So far all the news it is permissible to give is broadcast five or six times daily, and it is certain that so far as actual facts go, the man who turns the radio on at eight in the morning will learn more from it than he can from the paper just delivered at his door.

'Of course,' *The Spectator* continued, as if anxious to justify to its own readers the purpose it could serve, 'the papers have their own messages from centres like Washington and Paris, and various special features to which their readers are accustomed. Leading articles will still retain their value, but here, too, the Ministry of Information has taken to invading the field, unfortunately, as it seems to us. The issue, for example, by radio and through the Press of a comment on Goering's speech, introduced by the words, "it is considered in official circles that . . ." raises many questions. What are "official circles"? The Prime Minister? Lord Halifax? Some civil servant or other member of the Ministry of Information staff? We are not told.

'It is important that the Ministry of Information should publish facts, and as promptly and liberally as possible; whether it is desirable for it to circulate opinions is much more doubtful. Germans have for six years been told officially what to think. We have not, and are certainly not the worse for it.'

There was quite clearly a special challenge to which every journalist now had to address himself in order to satisfy his readers, and John Sayers, the President of the Institute of Journalists, quickly took the opportunity to urge his members to respond to the call. In a message issued on 4 September he said:

'Journalists are now, as they have always been, in the front line of the fight for freedom, and whether as combatants or in the exercise of their professional duties, which is itself national service of the first importance, all are ready to accept their share of a common duty. In war time, the Press, as a powerfully steadying influence, is an even greater asset than in times of peace. Its continuance is essential to the preservation of the public morale. The government is assured that journalists will remain faithful to their high sense of patriotic duty.'

In actual fact, the element that most threatened the continued publication of newspapers and all other periodicals during the war was not the dedication of journalists, but the shortage of raw material, the paper on which they were printed. Another factor that also immediately intruded was the dramatic fall in advertising as trade in most commodities slumped and manufacturers found themselves strapped for the extra cash needed for such promotions.

From the first week of September the national newspapers became thinner, although it was not until the summer of 1940 when Norway – one of the major sources of newsprint – was captured by the Germans, that paper actually became rationed.

The most famous of Britain's newspapers, *The Times*, managed to maintain much of its pre-war size of 8 to 10 pages by packing its columns with news and restricting its sales to certain of the most densely populated areas of the country. Of the popular press, the bed-sheet size *Daily Express*, varying in size from 16 to 24 pages in peace-time, had to cut back to as few as 6 by the middle of 1940, while the tabloid sized *Daily Mirror* managed to maintain its usual 8 pages for most of the time. London's famous evening papers, the *Evening Standard* and *The Star*, also appeared with 8 pages for much of the war – even through the devastation of the Blitz. To their credit, and that of their reporters and sub-editors, all the papers made the best use of their space, and their coverage of news was always comprehensive if sometimes brief.

Despite *The Spectator*'s exhortations to the press not to be subservient to the Ministry of Information, the newspapers as a whole chose not to criticize the Government too much and put their weight behind cheering up their readers and encouraging them to believe in victory. (The one exception to this was the communist *Daily Worker* which opposed the war effort and as a result was closed down for a time.) Reporting of the war was done factually and without embellishment, editorial comment usually being restricted to promoting national causes such as petrol rationing, food shortages and public morale. British eccentricity was, as ever, not neglected and stories such as that concerning the Commanding Officer who ordered all his

One of Low's acerbic cartoons for the Evening Standard.

THAT'S HIM! KILL HIM, BOY!

"Who Is Hitler?"

LONE MAN KNEW NOTHING OF CRISIS

LIVING in a wooden hut he built in a lonely lane in the village of Harlington, Middlesex, only ten miles from Charing Cross, is a man who knows nothing about Hitler or the crisis—grey-haired Henry Tillyer, aged 74.

Police were so worried for the safety of Harlington's "hermit" that recently they visited him and persuaded him to be fitted for a gas mask.

"I did not know what they were talking about," he told a "Star" man to-day, as he boiled a can of tea over a wood fire.

"I DON'T WANT A GAS MASK"

"But to satisfy them I went to a building in the village and was fitted with a mask. I have never seen one in my life before. They told me to take it away but I don't want it; and I left it there.

"It is 40 years since I first took to the open road. Since then I have always lived in the open and have been in this spot for five years.

"I am alone and do everything for myself. I get only my Old Age Pension. I cannot afford newspapers or wireless and mostly read the Bible.

BURNED HUT WAS HIS CRISIS

"Before I took to the road I was a prosperous builder, but my wife and I parted and it broke me up. I have heard folk talk of Hitler, but who is he and where does he live?

"I have heard nothing about a crisis, only the one I had a few weeks ago when my hut was burned down. That was the biggest crisis I have had in 40 years.

"All the pieces of furniture I had made and nick nacks I treasured were destroyed. I have only just finished building myself a new home."

From *The Star*, 30 August 1939

men to shout 'Hi-de-hi' when passing an officer, or the recluse who had never heard of Hitler (reproduced here) were always guaranteed to find space.

Naturally enough, humour – particularly that which poked fun at Germany and Hitler – was a staple feature in the nation's papers right from the day war was declared. Indeed, only a few days later the first of what was to prove a whole string of short-lived but none the less amusing comic papers, the *Daily Liar*, made its debut, being sold mainly in the street markets of London!

Columnists who brought a smile to their readers' faces were particularly popular, and foremost among these men were 'Beachcomber' (J. B. Morton) in the *Daily Express*, Timothy Shy in the *News Chronicle*, and – most famous of all – 'Nathaniel Gubbins' of the *Sunday Express* who became a national institution through his column 'Sitting on the Fence'. Gubbins, whose real name was the much more prosaic Edward Spencer, was known to millions of readers as 'Uncle

Nat' (though one of his critics insisted on calling him 'Dear Pig', an appellation to which he frequently made amused reference), and he delighted them all with weekly dialogues about characters such as his pessimistic cousin Florrie, Mr and Mrs Worm of Worms Avenue, 'Margaret's father', a kind of jingoistic Colonel Chinstrap, and – most beloved of all – Sally the Cat. Some typical items by Gubbins from his column on the Sunday that war broke out are included here as a fond reminder of 'the funniest man in newsprint', as Gubbins was widely known.

Cartoonists, too, came into their own in the war years, and the reputations of several were made at this time, including 'Vicky' of the *Daily Mirror*, Osbert Lancaster in the *Daily Express*, David Langdon, Nicholas Bentley, 'Fougasse' (Kenneth Bird) and Ernest H. Shepard, the man who had so delicately and charmingly illustrated *The Wind in the Willows* and now revealed himself as a hard-edged satirist of the Nazis.

The most famous strip-cartoon series throughout the war was undoubtedly the *Daily Mirror*'s adventures of Jane, the blonde with a habit of losing her clothes and forerunner of a whole gallery of such young ladies including today's 'Page 3 Girls'! The fewer clothes Jane was wearing – it was said – the better the effect on the morale of His Majesty's fighting forces who were her most avid fans. And by way of rewarding these men for all their efforts, the shapely young miss who had begun the war offering to display herself in a bikini at a beach show culminated her adventures by baring all on the day peace was declared!

For younger readers, Rupert the Bear continued his intrepid adventures in the *Daily Express*, seemingly unperturbed by events in the real world. Much the same could be said for the famous 'Fat Owl of the Remove', Billy Bunter, who appeared each week in *The Magnet*, although by the winter of 1939 Greyfriars School was enduring the blackout. Sadly, this now much-collected comic did not survive the war, publication ceasing with the July 1940 issue. By contrast, another hero of schoolchildren, Richmal Crompton's incorrigible William, became very much caught up in

The Daily Mirror*'s Jane, the strip-cartoon heroine (in more ways than one!) who was the forerunner of the modern 'Page 3 Girls' and was a great favourite with the forces throughout the war – ultimately rewarding her fans by baring all on the day victory was announced!*

events, one of his most popular adventures being *William and the ARP* which appeared in the autumn of 1939.

The popular *Boy's Own Paper* devoted a considerable amount of space to the ways in which its readers could 'do their bit' for the country, and advised those who had 'brothers fighting for Britain against bullying aggression' to 'take heart' for there were many good men looking out for their welfare. 'I know, chaps,' the editor said in one of his 'Yarns While the Dixie Boils', 'for I went through it all last time.' A typical BOP article, 'Helping the ARP', is reproduced on page 155.

Astrology and horoscope columns continued to appear in both newspapers and magazines, endeavour-

'Giles', who was to become a household name, busied himself in the early months of the war with propaganda posters such as this one for the 'war' against germs!

ing to predict better times ahead for their readers. That they were still read at all after the appalling gaffe by one of the most famous of their number, 'Lyndoe' of *The People*, who predicted in his Sunday column of 3 September that there would be no war, is perhaps to be marvelled at!

Elsewhere in the pages of the national press, other familiar features were still to be found. The 'agony aunt' of the *Daily Sketch*, for instance, was still answering one of the world's most pressing problems, war or no war. Under the heading 'Bust Enlargement', the columnist informed 'Mary of Brighton' on 5 Sept-

ember: 'It is very difficult to enlarge the bust by any external application; the best and healthiest way of achieving this is by exercise. All the deep-breathing exercises are good, particularly the one which involves rising on the toes and at the same time raising the arms straight above the head and bringing them back in a circle to your sides, keeping the shoulders as far back as they will go. Swimming also helps to develop the bust. Also wear a good brassiere with the uplift line which takes away the flat-chested look.'

Other readers were asking their papers about matters of more immediacy such as the cost of living, and a

GREYFRIARS TO THE RESCUE!

The MAGNET
Billy Bunter's Own Paper
2D

No. 1,646. Vol. LVI.　　　EVERY SATURDAY.　　　Week Ending September 2nd, 1939.

HELPING THE A.R.P.

● Jobs that You Can Do

THERE are plenty of ways in which you can be useful in helping the A.R.P., and really to be helping is not just good fun—it can be that—but is fine citizenship and service too.

If you want to help, as of course you do, you can begin right away. Plenty of things need attention before the air-raid warning sounds, and everyone, besides the officials, has a part to play. In your own street or village or district you can be either someone who simply doesn't matter or one who earns respect and liking by thoughtful service and cheerful energy. This world is going to need a lot of building up into peace and happiness again, and it will want good men to do it. Now is the time to train yourself and develop the sort of character that will count so much in the happier days ahead.

But let's get down to brass-tacks. What can you do? First, make the acquaintance of your nearest A.R.P. warden. You can easily find him by the plate on his house. It's pretty certain he'll be glad to know he can call on you for any little odd jobs he needs doing, and he may give you tips on things you can do right away. Probably he's a busy man, so don't worry him unduly; but in any emergency take care to be on hand if he thinks he will be able to use you.

You must study also the whole local A.R.P. arrangements—the auxiliary fire service, the first-aid posts, and so on. It ought to be fairly easy to make the acquaintance of members of the various services and learn all you can from them of their duties.

Then be sure the A.R.P. arrangements in your own home and the homes of your friends are in tip-top order. Even now the black-outs of houses are not always as thorough as they might be, and many people still make shift with very troublesome, improvised arrangements—bits of cardboard which have to be fastened up afresh with drawing-pins each evening, and

by SID G. HEDGES

that sort of thing. You may be able to help by sticking strips of brown paper down the edges of glass panes, where the dangerous strips of light so often appear; screwing in proper hooks for curtains to hang on; painting black the sides of light shades nearest to windows. Occasionally do a round of the houses after dark, looking for light spots that require fresh attention.

The construction of shelters may also give you the chance of a bit of strenuous labour. All people haven't made provision against danger yet. Perhaps someone is just waiting for the bit of digging that you might do to fix up a snug trench in the garden. No doubt you know something of how such a trench should be constructed—wider at top than bottom; sides boarded or shored up; height not less than 6 feet if it is roofed over; if possible a wooden slatting to walk on, with narrow drainage channel underneath; banked earth or sandbags, perhaps a couple of feet deep on top; entrances zigzagged or at right-angles to the main trench; a seat along one or both walls—dependent on the trench width. Even if all this has been done you may tidy things up, perhaps taking away outer ugliness by turfing the roof over.

Make a study of house interiors. All people ought to know the safest spot in their home, if they are not able to get out to other shelter. The important thing is to be protected on every side by the greatest number of walls, and to have the smallest span of ceiling overhead. Of course, the best spot is always on the ground floor. Often it is in a narrow passage, the end which is near the middle of the house. There is less likelihood of the narrow span of ceiling collapsing than when the ceiling stretches right across a wide room. If a ceiling can be shored up by stout timbers so that it is supported

---

Billy Bunter continued his popular escapades at Greyfriars as if there were no war on – until fate brought The Magnet *to a close in July 1940.*

Magazines such as the Boy's Own Paper *encouraged their young readers to help out in the war effort with articles like this one in the September 1939 issue.*

Daily Telegraph columnist gave this helpful answer to one of her correspondents on 7 September: 'You will indeed find a difference in the cost of housekeeping now. If you wish to serve breakfast with one "dish", a two-course luncheon, and two or three course dinner, all simple fare, you would need to allow about 15 shillings per head per week. Laundry for three persons (all sent out) might account for a further 7s 6d to 10s weekly, depending on the amount sent and type of article (lace-trimmed silk garments are charged more than cotton; linen sheets cost more to wash than cotton).'

As far as *The Lady*'s correspondence columns were concerned, there might almost have been no war on at all – as readers continued to seek advice on problems as diverse as preserving beans in salt, mixing cocktails, the wages of housekeepers, and whether a fashion was likely to develop among ladies for wearing cowboy boots! Under the heading 'Table Manners', the following delightful advice was also proffered: 'One may say that it is not "etiquette" to take anything unpleasant into the mouth; one should eat in such a way as to avoid doing so. If something must be removed it is best to do so as inconspicuously as possible, and therefore not with a fork, but with the thumb and first finger.'

All the newspapers and magazines carried on their 'Letters to the Editor' pages, and despite the restrictions on space, most editors' post bags were obviously as full as ever. The war was naturally the dominating topic in a great many of these, but unusual subjects still found their place in those first weeks of September. My favourite among all those I came across was the following letter to *The Times* of 7 September under the heading 'Crosswords':

'Sir, I hope that the manufacture of crosswords will be regarded as work of national importance and their ingenious authors not claimed for other service. What a boon they would have been in the last war! What better to fill in the inevitable lacunae of a martial career or the weary hours in hospital? May we ask that henceforth and for "the duration" the clues should rely on wit and not give way overmuch to Dictionary references. Perhaps it would be possible to confine clues to the words in the *Little Oxford Dictionary* which, although surprisingly comprehensive, can be easily slipped in the pocket or haversack.'

The letter is signed 'Lieutenant-Colonel H. P. Garwood, Hurlingham Court'.

British wit being what it is, the war soon began to produce a whole new crop of jokes, and these, too, rapidly found their way into the pages of the newspapers and magazines. The *Radio Times* actually claimed 'The First Laugh of the War', reporting in its second wartime issue, 'On 5 September an announcer was heard to say in his usual clear voice, "We are now to hear dance music played by Victor Sylvester and his Bathroom Orchestra."'

The *Daily Mirror*, however, was the first newspaper to run a weekly column of war humour called 'Nazi Nuggets', although *The Star* was almost as quickly off the mark to offer its readers 'Asterisks' which contained such first-week gems as: 'Knitting soothes the nerves – don't lose your wool'; 'Germans already on food rations – inside information' and 'Today's misprint – She worked in a night-shift'.

The blackout proved the first major source of inspiration for humour, and the *News Chronicle* ran a column entitled 'Heard in the Black-Out' which invited contributions from readers and paid 2s 6d for every submission used. An early prize-winner ran thus: 'Air-Raid Warden to woman of loose morals: "There's a chink showing in your window" – "Mind your own business, I'll entertain my gentlemen friends whatever their nationality!"' Another anecdote concerned the girl who was overhead saying, as she travelled in a blacked-out train, 'Take your hand off my knee – Not you . . . *You!*'

Time & Tide magazine similarly devoted a spot each week to Cockney humour. Here is a typical item from the issue of 2 September.

'The current situation is inevitably a subject for comment by the woman who cleans my flat every morning. Last Monday found her pessimistic.

'"This Hitler," she said, "was a painter and decorator, wasn't he?" I said he was. "Hm," she said, "so's my husband, they're all the same."'

The best source of all for humour was undoubtedly *Punch* – just as it had been through the previous war with its splendid mixture of humorous writing and comic illustrations. Always topical, the magazine very much mirrored the British sense of humour and indomitable spirit, amusing its readers from the very day war broke out with such little gems as these from its 'Charivaria' page:

'A fine summer is promised for 1940. There is plenty of cheering news about if you only look for it.'

'"Herr Hitler would have made an excellent journalist," we read. Even now it is highly unlikely that any Berlin editor would turn down his stuff.'

'Germans are said to visit their dentists more often than most people. Probably because the dentist's surgery is the only place where a German can open his mouth and get away with it.'

'There are many public statues in out-of-the-way corners of London, says a writer. In our opinion they should be moved to places of danger.'

'However long the war lasts, we read, there will be no shortage of tinned beef. That's bully!'

SITTING ON THE FENCE

BY
NATHANIEL GUBBINS

"WELL," said The Sweep, "I see by the papers that little old Itler was losin that there war of nerves. But it don't seem like it now, do it?"

"It don't," I said.

"All the same," said The Sweep, "I see the pore little chap aint been to bed till five o'clock in the morning for the larst week. So he might lose it yet."

"That's right," I said.

"And then he's up again at seven talking to little old von Ribbondrops. Cor crickey, fancy gittin up at seven to talk to im."

"Fancy," I said.

"Cor stone me blimey," said The Sweep, "I'd sooner stay in bed and talk to meself."

"Same ere," I said.

Letter From An Aunt

MY Dear Boy,

Poor darling Porgy is winning the war of nerves against Hitler—he eats his biscuits and chicken liver every day and has been burying more bones in the garden since he heard hoarding was allowed—I am trying to organise ration cards for dogs if anything happens—I thought of a card to be tied round their necks with the words "Doggies Have Tummies Too"—then they could queue up at the butchers by themselves.

*   *   *

Of course Emily has been very unBritish about everything—she wanted to live in the Cheddar Caves until the gardener, who was in the last war, told her that a bomb would get her anywhere if it had her name on it—as I told her, it was absurd to suppose that Hitler had nothing better to do than to write her name on a bomb and order somebody to get Emily wherever she is—I don't suppose Hitler has ever heard of Emily, and anyway, as I said, she might just as well be blown to pieces as catch her death of cold in a damp cave.

*   *   *

Florrie came round to tea and told us the Germans have a new gas which doesn't work for a week—she said they would come over only once and drop the gas bombs, and just when we thought the war was over we should all drop dead—of course, this sent Emily into hysterics and we had to send for the doctor, who said Emily ought to have been married years ago, though I can't see what that's got to do with it.

*   *   *

I don't think your Uncle Fred will ever get over the Russian pact—first he thought that Hitler was a bulwark against Bolshevism, then he thought Russia was a bulwark against Hitler—now his only hope is Mussolini, though the gardener, who was in one of the British divisions sent to help the Italians after Caporetto, says it's much safer to have Italy on the other side.

Anyway, your Uncle Fred is glad that the Poles are gentlemen—except their lower classes, of course—and are mostly sound Conservatives and good churchgoers.

Your loving

AUNT MAUD.

Conversation With Sally The Cat

"ITHINK you might have shown a more generous spirit towards the two refugee cats who were brought to the Nest for safety."

"I refuse to have anything to do with cats of that class."

"In that case you might have ignored them. But to slap their faces and chase them into the next garden was not only inhospitable, it was an unnecessary piece of hooliganism which reveals a mean and ugly nature masked beneath a benevolent and, if I may say so, extremely charming exterior."

"Do you have to make a speech about it?"

"I feel very strongly on such matters. What would you think of me if I slapped visitors' faces and chased them out of the house?"

"I should mind my own business."

"In times like this we must try to help each other regardless of personal tastes and prejudices. Tomorrow I expect to see you and the refugee cat eating and drinking from the same saucer."

"You're in for a disappointment."

"Do you mean to say you won't?"

"I'll starve to death first."

"So you're nothing but a miserable little snob?"

"If refusing to eat with guttersnipe alley cats is snobbery, then I am a snob. Besides, the kittens are reaching an impressionable age, and one can't be too careful."

"What do you expect these poor little cats to do, then?"

"Go back to where they belong."

"And run the risk of being bombed?"

"What's wrong with that? They both look as if they ought to be destroyed, anyway."

"Sure, you are so class-conscious it seems a pity you are not more particular in the choice of husbands."

"I beg your pardon?"

"If ever there was a low type cat it's that flat-eared, battle-scarred horror who is the father of your children."

"I refuse to stay here and listen to insults."

"You don't have to stay. You can get back to your alley kittens."

"I hope the crisis has not affected your nerves. You sound a little overtired."

"I don't want any of that stuff from you."

"Perhaps when you are in a calmer frame of mind we can discuss differences of opinion without losing our tempers."

"Get out of here."

WANTED: ARTIFICIAL TEETH

It has been said that the Classified Advertisements sections in daily newspapers and magazines reveal more about the character of a nation than all the news carried in those publications' pages. If this is true – and there is evidence to support the case – then the columns of 'small ads' which appeared in the British press in the first week of September 1939 reveal a people torn between great generosity and unashamed opportunism!

Indeed, in looking through the pages of these journals – and picking classifieds as varied as those found in *The Times*' famous 'Personal' column to those in *Amateur Gardening* – it is possible to discover an amazing variety of offers couched in every style from the authoritative to the begging, not to mention the amusing! Unfortunately, space only permits me to include a small selection of some of those which particularly caught my eye – but the reader may rest assured that they are typical of a great many more! As those offering property in the 'safe zones' are by far the most prolific at this time, I have started with them . . .

*

IN THE EVENT OF WAR would let small furnished country house, 4 bedrooms, 2 receptions, good garden, main electricity.
The Times, September 1

*

SAFE HOTEL. Royal Victoria, St. Leonard's-on-Sea. 60 Beds, restaurant and lounge. Ballroom and adjacent toilets have been made gas and splinter-proof.
The Tatler, September 2

*

CHOOSE YOUR OWN SAFETY ZONE! Full size buses to live in; existing seats make excellent beds; electric light; £55 each, deliver anywhere.
The *Sunday Times*, September 3

*

BE SAFE AND COMFORTABLE in yacht lying in small river near Ipswich, Suffolk, accommodate six–eight, all furnishings.
The *Daily Mail*, September 5

*

CELLARS, spacious, dry, solid; excellent large house above. London 20 miles.
The *Daily Telegraph*, September 6

*

LIVE PEACEFULLY in Sussex free of worries. Tunbridge Wells property invisible from the air.
Country Life, September 8

*

SCHOOL being formed in very safe country district for boys up to 16 from preparatory and public schools.
The Times, September 2

*

PARENTS who wish may send girls back AT ONCE. Lindores School, Bexhill-on-Sea.
The *Daily Telegraph*, September 4

*

MR. EVELYN WAUGH wishes to let Piers Court near Dursley, Glos. Furnished for duration of war. Old house recently modernised; 4 reception, 10 bed, 4 bath, etc. 4 acres or more. Low rent to civilised tenant.
The Times, September 8

*

NOW is the time to think of Autumn Holidays. Greenbank Hotel, Falmouth.
Time & Tide, September 9

*

FLOODLIGHTING of public buildings, churches & etc carried out by experienced Liverpool company.
The Builder, September 1

*

VICAR of large country parish, now Head Warden ARP, would be grateful for an old car.
The *Christian Herald*, September 9

*

CHAUFFEUR-DRIVE LUXURY LIMOUSINES for hire only 6d per mile. Davis-Turner Motors.
City Press, September 8

*

AMBULANCE FOR DOGS. Our motor ambulance has done seven years service to sick and injured dogs. Please help us get a new one.
The *Daily Sketch*, September 6

*

EVACUATE DOGS for holiday to neutral territory. Ten shillings a week, gun dogs £1. Donegal.
Country Life, September 8

*

LOST. Black Scottish Terrier answering to the name of 'Teddy' during air raid alarm 3 a.m. on Monday in Princes Gate. Reward.
The *Daily Telegraph*, September 6

*

ELAINE. Hope your strange adventure ended happily. E.W.
The Times, September 5

BREED RABBITS. Safeguard your larder. Three breeding Does produce nearly 2cwt carcases per annum. Crawley, Sussex.
Amateur Gardening, September 8

*

UNWANTED ARTIFICIAL TEETH gratefully received.
The *Daily Herald*, September 4

*

CLUB with BLAST and SPLINTER-PROOF dining room – all enquires for special membership. Albany Club.
Burlington Magazine, September 1

*

SUNNINGDALE GOLF CLUB. Members and others are notified that as from Monday 4th September 1939, no meals will be available in the club house.
The *Sunday Times*, September 3

*

MISS DOUGLAS-LOCKHART wishes to announce that the De Vere Club remains open. Rooms available as usual; refuge room. Kensington.
The Times, September 5

*

JIG-SAW PUZZLE CLUB. For particulars write to the Secretary, Kenwyn House, Barnstaple.
The *Daily Express*, September 8

*

PARLOUR MAID. Can any lady closing house in danger zone recommend good Parlour Maid for country house in Breconshire?
The Lady, September 8

*

WILL ANYONE please give young man a chance to redeem himself? Accept any post anywhere. Neat, adaptable, energetic worker, experienced several trades, office work, typewriting, shopkeeping, advertising, journalism. Box 248.
The Times, September 8

*

WILL true Christian help another by buying Legacy of £1,000 for £650? URGENT. Box K125.
The Times, September 6

*

ARE YOU GOING ABROAD? If so, send a postcard to Publisher of *The Times*, Printing House Square, London E.C.4., for subscription rates.
The Times, September 4

An advertisement from Time & Tide, *2 September 1939.*

Liverpool looking peaceful under the cover of a barrage balloon – though rumour claimed that the city had been attacked by German bombers not long after the declaration of war!

14 Tittle-Tattle Lost the Battle

Rumours flourished as never before among a people renowned for their love of gossip in the hours which followed the declaration of war. Unsure of precisely *what* would happen in the aftermath of Chamberlain calling Hitler's bluff, the people of the British Isles in many cases simply invented the news they were not given.

Contemporary accounts indicate that the maximum period of rumour was immediately following three false alarms of air raids given on 3, 4 and 6 September. According to these stories, nearly every town of importance in Britain had been 'bombed to ruins' while hundreds of eye-witnesses claimed to have 'seen' aircraft falling from the skies in flames. The strength of these rumours was further underlined by the undisputed fact that on at least two occasions anti-aircraft units had actually opened fire on their own planes!

Although the vast majority of rumours that proliferated in the country can be put down to a collective case of nerves once war had been confirmed, along with a lack of official news, the widespread nature and variety of them is still astonishing. For example, on the Sunday afternoon – according to a story circulating throughout much of south-east England – a German plane had allegedly crash-landed near Woolwich. Another version of the story said the location was Essex (Chingford, Chigwell and Goodmayes were favoured spots) where the aircraft was found to be painted to look like an English aircraft! Popular gossip even had a third version that the plane *was* actually British and had failed to reach its home base after a sortie over Germany to drop propaganda leaflets, where it was damaged by enemy fire.

The following morning, another story gaining wide credibility was that the first German air raid had been directed at Winchester (of all places!) leaving 35 people dead and twice as many injured. Ilford, near London, was also supposed to have been bombed in the early hours (by the German planes returning home from Winchester?), although gossip insisted that several of the raiders had been shot down in the Woodford area.

A third extraordinary report said the first German air raid on Britain had occurred on the Tuesday night and had been carried out in an old Zeppelin! This had apparently been brought down over Kent and the crew of 23 men were now being held in Canterbury where anyone who disbelieved the story could go and see them in prison!

Perhaps the strongest of all the early rumours concerned a supposed air raid on the city of Liverpool. Gossips insisted that a squadron of about ten German bombers had suddenly appeared over the Mersey, following the line of the river. An anti-aircraft battery near the mouth had opened fire and was then supported by other units, resulting in the planes turning back – although at least three were said to have been badly damaged and forced to land at an airport just outside Liverpool.

Though no word of this bravely resisted 'raid' was mentioned either in the press or on the radio, the story was still persisting two weeks later when the *Daily Express* columnist William Hickey visited the city. Naturally intrigued when he heard the tale, Hickey made enquiries and found a probable and quite different explanation of the events. It seemed that three heavy RAF bombers had been flying near the city when they were spotted from a distance by a nervous citizen who quickly spread a panic rumour that Liverpool had been caught unawares by a lightning raid! Even when disproved, however, such tales still continued to retain widespread currency and were, in turn, the fathers of other still more spectacular rumours.

The author and columnist Naomi Royde-Smith became an avid collector of such wartime gossip, retelling some of the best stories that came her way in her contributions to *Time & Tide* magazine. One early yarn again featured Winchester. This rumour maintained that the lovely old community would never be bombed by the Germans because Hitler had decided that after he had conquered England he would be crowned in the city's cathedral! Why the Fuehrer should have preferred Winchester to Westminster Abbey was not disclosed, and though Miss Royde-Smith said nobody believed the story, 'everybody spoke of it'. In a later column she discussed a number of other equally absurd rumours that had come her way:

'Another tale told as a secret about giant guns mounted on the Brocken and trained on London which would, in half an hour, demolish the capital, I have traced to the ingenious pen of Mr Bernard Newman; in much the same way as the nine deaths or disappearances of Hitler must have sprung from Mr Peter Fleming's *Flying Visit*. The legend of the Siegfried Line, hastily built of undried and therefore friable concrete, has now gone back into the circulating library fiction from which it sprang. Every institution was going somewhere else at this time. Westminster was coming to Winchester (again!); Harrow was going to Cheltenham; no-one was going to Cambridge; and the Cabinet had gone to Canada in a Yankee Clipper.'

And in an attempt to demonstrate just how absurd she considered the vast majority of these rumours, Miss Royde-Smith related an absolute classic. 'Our best rumour,' she wrote, 'was a real sensation. One morning I noticed a distant smell of hot onions. As I was repainting chairs at the time I thought this might be due to some war economy in the composition of the enamel I was using – or that the onions had been added to the cheese and cocoa which the daily woman requires with her elevenses. An hour later I went off to have my hair shampooed and learnt that there had been a gas alarm from Southampton. Air-Raid Wardens, in gas masks, had paraded the town, school-

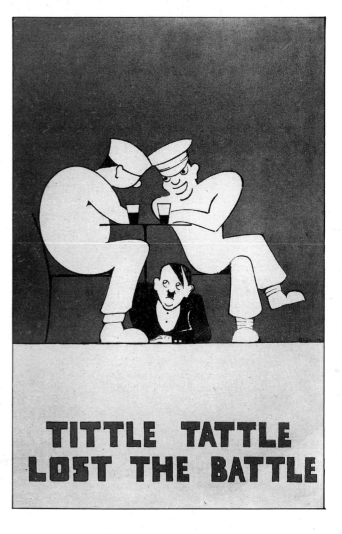

A poster widely displayed at the start of the war to discourage careless gossiping.

children had been put into their gas masks; the hair dresser had been told to close all the windows and warn his clients to keep their heads well into the basins. The agitation was at its height when a message came through to say that the pollution of the atmosphere was not of Enemy Origin. A local pickle factory had had a fire and onions and vinegar frying and boiling together had produced a miasma blown by the wind in our direction!'

Not all the rumours that flew about Britain during the early days of September were as laughable – or harmless – as that one, however. And the authorities, quickly realizing they had underestimated the public need for information and their ingenuity at making it up when so denied, took several courses of action.

On the radio, a number of broadcasts were initiated to quell public apprehension and try to stop rumour-mongering. A former spy, described only as 'E.7.', talked perhaps a little too melodramatically about the dangers of gossiping, in a programme he called 'Take Care What You Say!': 'I'm a spy,' he told his audience on the night of 6 September, 'or perhaps I should say I *was* – an international spy – though, being British too, I've never worked, of course, against the home country. Why I've come along now is to tell you from the inside the sort of things spies can make use of, so that you won't go giving away information that might be valuable without your knowing it.'

After a somewhat guarded discussion about his own past work and a description of the typical spy as being far removed from the traditional idea of a man with a beard and slouch hat or a ravishing blonde *femme fatale*, E.7. summarized his advice to listeners: 'First of all, a remark that seems perfectly harmless and that is uttered in all good faith may cause immense harm in these days. Remember that a secret shared, no matter with whom, is no longer a secret. Secondly, just because you have listened to this talk, don't get the wind up and suspect every stranger you meet. Just use your common sense. Finally, the only way that I can see of dealing with the problem – for it is a problem and a very serious one – is to say nothing at all about your work to anyone – *not even your wife!*'

As a kind of antidote to E.7.'s dramatics, the well-known poet and essayist John Pudney tried satirizing the gossip in a series of talks, one of which, 'The Rumour Man', attracted such interest that it was published in *The Listener* of 21 September and is reprinted opposite.

The press also did their best to scotch the worst rumours – the *Daily Mirror* actually launching an emotively worded campaign against what it called the 'Scaremongers' who should be avoided like smallpox cases! In a prominently displayed editorial on Monday

4 September (also reproduced on these pages) the paper urged its readers to disbelieve alarmist gossip, not to pass on information about military installations, and above all to keep smiling. 'Be silent, be discreet, enemy ears are listening to you,' the *Mirror* urged in its inimitable way.

On behalf of the Government, the Ministry of Information, whose prime job was to sustain civilian morale during wartime and which had been brought into existence with this objective in mind as early as 1936, began a number of campaigns to raise public spirits using posters and slogans. Many of these remained familar long after the hostilities were over. One of the earliest campaigns featured a brilliant series of posters entitled 'Careless Talk Costs Lives' and drawn by the *Punch* cartoonist 'Fougasse' (Kenneth Bird). With sub-headings such as 'Don't forget that walls have ears!' and 'Strictly between these four walls', the pictures underlined the anti-gossip campaign, though there were critics who felt that they tended to reinforce a prevailing belief that there were spies and informers *everywhere*.

A not dissimilar campaign consisted of two posters showing either a man's or a woman's hat with the words 'Keep it under Your Hat! – Careless Talk Costs Lives'.

John Pudney's revealing satire on gossip from The Listener, *21 September 1939.*

The Rumour Man

A Parable by JOHN PUDNEY

'MR. WHYSOP says that the noise in the night was the Czechs landing at Birmingham in parachutes. He says he is quite sure of this because he says his sister-in-law knows a man in Macclesfield who was asked about an order for the silk for a million parachutes'.

'Mr. Whysop told my husband that the French had sent us a huge store of tinned frogs. He heard about it in Boulogne, you know. He was over there for the day when he was on his summer holidays'.

'But did you hear what Mr. Whysop said about that Mrs. B. whose son married a German girl? Mr. Whysop thinks the boy has really given up the estate agency business to become something to do with that Dr. Gobble's propaganda. . . . Mr. Whysop thinks he is only pretending to be an estate agent'.

Now, let me say frankly: Away with Mr. Whysop.

Regard this George Whysop, of the long ears, and the ginger moustache, twitching with rumour. They do say that he is a retired ironmonger, released from a slightly insolvent business by the convenient death of a moneyed aunt. Regard him, in these late summer days, with his white linen jacket, his panama hat, and his curious walkingstick, passing the time of day on his way to the shops.

It was Mr. Whysop, if I remember rightly, who came to realise that South Africa and South America were once joined together in one continent. He could explain in detail, given the time, how a great eruption had severed them, leaving them both, he would add, with the same snakes. This made a profound impression in its time, for it occurred between the Derby and Ascot: and as Mr. Whysop never displayed the second-hand pseudo-scientific mag. from which he obtained the story, it was thought to have been the result of his own research. It is easy, you see, for Mr. Whysop, with an inquisitive mind and time on his hands, to *acquire* knowledge.

I assure you, he *has* been right. He was right when he said that the lady with the foreign name would do a moonlight flit from the Grange. He was right when he said it would rain in the evening of Coronation Day. He *may* have been right when he said that, while crossing on a day excursion steamer to Boulogne last year, he saw Ludendorff in uniform drinking beer. He may have been right when he said he saw the French, during his visit, building a vast tunnel beneath the harbour in the direction of England.

There is some slight doubt about his suggestion that Miss K., having been a land girl in the last war, was therefore addicted to cigars. For it was noticed that she was nearly ill after smoking a single cigarette at a whist drive. He may have been wrong, too, about the death of Mrs. Oliver's cat being foul play by someone in the house, about the marriage laws of Japan, about the unemployed, about the Loch Ness monster having been inflated with a bicycle pump in a garage at Inverness.

These vital questions, from time to time, were harrowed by his rumour-sharp moustache, were ploughed by the shares of his industrious tongue, were husbanded by his wide, all-hearing ears. Residents in the suburb miss George Whysop when he goes for his annual holiday on the South Coast. He fills in the corners of people's lives, he keeps out the draughts of boredom, he adds rumours to rumours, and embroiders, with his sallow threads of imagination, the familiar everyday scenes.

But to some of us, Mr. Whysop is not the joke he used to be. He grappled with the war as soon as it came. A war delights him, his rumour-sharp moustache, his inquisitive ears. . . .

So let us remember, now, that he has never seen a German, even on his day excursion to Boulogne, that he doesn't know the difference between a British and a German aeroplane, that he knows nobody—not even on the Urban District Council, much less in a Government Department—that he once went to school and was considered stupid, that he once went to business and was a failure, that he is known to be stupid now . . . but that that stupidity does not make him dumb.

Take a bow, Mr. Whysop.

Take the air, Mr. Whysop.

But, oh Mr. Whysop, take a few days off somewhere now that we have a war.

This was certainly more aesthetically pleasing than four more posters declaring in huge black type 'WARNING – Do not discuss anything which might be of National Importance. THE CONSEQUENCE OF ANY SUCH INDISCRETION MAY BE THE LOSS OF MANY LIVES'

Later came one of the most ingenious of all the Ministry's poster campaigns, which coined the phrase 'Silent Column' and used male and female models to show six typical unpatriotic citizens much addicted to promoting rumour and gossip: 'Mr Secrecy Hush Hush', 'Mr Knowall', 'Miss Leaky Mouth', 'Miss Teacup Whisper', 'Mr Pride in Prophecy' and 'Mr Glumpot'.

In fact, gossiping was so much a part of the national character that to stop it was virtually impossible, and even the introduction in 1940 of a law forbidding the passing on of any rumour likely to cause 'alarm and despondency' and carrying a fine of up to £50 or a month in prison could not still the wagging tongues. The *Daily Herald*, in commenting on a Ministry of Information instruction to citizens actually to try to stop people listening to rumours, said it would result in 'a large number of us walking about with black eyes and the police worked to death!'.

For the authorities, the problem of rumour and gossip was to persist throughout the entire war, and more than one commentator has observed that it was precisely *because* there were so many people who didn't believe what they heard on the radio or read in their newspapers that it remained a major phenomenon all this time. Writing about this in his book *War Begins at Home* (1940), Tom Harrison of the Mass Observation Unit said, 'Rumour makes people sceptical about conflicting versions, and thus about any version, including the official one. This process was already far advanced in this country a week after war started. The war, which had started in an aura of emptiness, became a kind of series of collective hallucinations. The rumours were projections of the fears and wishes in the minds of the masses.'

Of all the stories of rumours which circulated at the start of the war, there is one that nicely illustrates the country's state of mind at that time. It was related by the writer of the column 'A London Diary' in the *New Statesman* of 9 September.

'Most of us have stories of "how we saw the war in", but I doubt if anyone in this country had a more bizarre experience than my friend who was at a large holiday camp. Throughout the crisis, the camp authorities refused to broadcast any news and maintained that all war-talk was "just rumour". It was, my friend remarked, a regime of totalitarian high spirits.

'On the Friday when Poland was invaded, the two thousand odd campers in the two great dining rooms were informed by the stentorian loud speaker that, in spite of all gossip, the camp was definitely carrying on. "Heigh-de-he," shouted the unseen leader. "Heigh-de-ho," replied the two thousand, and, clasping their hands above their heads, thundered the camp song in cheery defiance of war.

'There is no doubt this censorship of politics was a great relief. News bulletins are a drug, my friend assures me, and he was better without them, although he did on occasion slip furtively out of the camp and lurk outside a private house to catch the news. But, alas! the charmed circle was broken on Friday evening.

'At 4 a.m. the holiday-makers were awakened by reveille and my friend's last glimpse of the camp was a smartly dressed officer scanning the crowd of bathing belles and anxious mothers and remarking loudly, "Won't be so bad here when we get these dreadful people out!"'

DON'T . . .

THIS is intended for YOU. Read it, remember it, pass it on to your friends. First, and most important of all things is

Don't Listen to Rumours

You will get all the news that matters—bad or good—in your newspapers. Disbelieve anything else you hear—particularly alarmist news. Next thing to remember is

Don't Broadcast Information

You may know that there is an anti-aircraft gun cunningly concealed in the field next to your garden. But that's no reason for passing on the information. It may reach someone who should not know it.

Don't Lose Your Head

IN OTHER WORDS—KEEP SMILING. THERE'S NOTHING TO BE GAINED BY GOING ABOUT WITH THE CORNERS OF YOUR MOUTH TURNED DOWN: AND IT HAS A BAD EFFECT ON PEOPLE WHOSE NERVES ARE NOT SO GOOD AS YOURS.

SO EVEN IF A BOMB FALLS IN YOUR STREET—WHICH IS UNLIKELY—KEEP SMILING.

Don't Listen to Scaremongers

You will always find scaremongers about. Just treat them as you would a smallpox case—move on quickly. The enemy loves to spread rumours. Part of his campaign was to panic Britain—and he will still try it, hopeless although it is.

Don't Cause Crowds to Assemble

THE POLICE HAVE ENOUGH TO DO. IF YOU SEE PEOPLE GATHERING AND THERE IS NO REASON FOR YOU TO JOIN THEM—WALK ON. IN OTHER WORDS—MIND YOUR OWN BUSINESS.

AND ABOVE ALL DON'T FORGET THE OLD ARMY ADAGE.

Be silent, be discreet, enemy ears are listening to you.

NOW GET AHEAD, DO YOUR JOB AND DON'T WORRY.

From the *Daily Mirror*, 4 September 1939

15 Love Makes the World Go Round

DARLING – cheer up. We shall be together sooner than you think despite this. Love – G.

An advertisement from the personal column of *The Times*, 2 September.

The one thing that the war could not put a stop to was love. Though death and destruction threatened the nation, nothing was going to be allowed to dull the passion between men and women – regardless of whether it was open or illicit. The records reveal that engagements and marriages flourished at the onset of the hostilities, and by the end of the year more couples had been wed in Great Britain than for many a year previously. Indeed, the total number of marriages for 1939, 495,000, was almost 100,000 up on 1938. (The following year, 1940, was to see an all-time peak of 534,000!)

THE MARRIAGE RACE

Hundreds of young couples flocked to the principal register offices in London on Saturday to give notice of marriage and to try to arrange the earliest possible date for the ceremony.

From the *News Chronicle*, 4 September 1939

Undoubtedly the uncertainty about the future and the very strong possibility of being separated was uppermost in the minds of all young men and women who were in love. Although during the summer months many engaged couples had been busy trying to convince themselves – and anyone else who might listen – that 'This is no time to marry' or 'This is no world into which to bring children', during the first days of September churches throughout the nation reported a bumper crop of weddings, while queues were actually to be seen outside many register offices as men and women – some already in service uniforms – were married.

For many brides there was little time to make a white wedding dress – indeed, during the early weeks of the war such a dress was considered rather showy, if not actually unpatriotic, because of the general shortage of materials – while for bridegrooms there was the problem of finding a best man when many of his friends might already have been called up. A further headache was buying a ring, for such was the demand that many jewellers sold out, and with the government restrictions on gold the best that most could find were nine-carat 'utility' rings.

The ceremonies themselves were often hastily performed by clergy or registry officials nervous of the threat of an air raid: and it became a widespread superstition during the war that if a siren actually sounded during the ceremony, the marriage was doomed to failure.

Cruelly, two of the most cherished traditions of the wedding ceremony were stopped by the war. First, it was made illegal to manufacture confetti because of the paper shortage, or to throw rice at the couple (real flower petals were substituted when available); and secondly, as sugar was in short supply, it was forbidden to ice wedding cakes: chocolate coverings were suggested as a rather odd-looking alternative! Interestingly, because of the food shortage, wedding gifts of sugar, butter and jam were by far and away the most acceptable presents many couples received.

The wedding announcement columns of newspapers such as *The Times* and the *Daily Telegraph* overflowed for days with details of matches that had taken place suddenly 'owing to the declaration of war' or even 'owing to the cancellation of leave'. Honeymoons, it was said, would of necessity have to wait for more peaceful times, though there were some couples 'fortunate' enough to snatch a few days together if they were prepared to spend their nights in air-raid shelters!

The tremendous increase in weddings equally predictably led to a baby boom. Many couples, afraid that the war might result in the death of one or other of them (the fear of dying in a bombing raid on England was just as real as that of being killed on a field of battle somewhere abroad), made conscious efforts to have offspring before they were parted. As a child born in April 1940 myself, my mother has told me: 'Of course it was a risk having you when the war was on, but I wanted something of your father if he did not come back.' (In fact, my father was posted abroad with the RAF, served in Egypt, and did not return home until I was almost five years old. Delighted as I was to see this strange man I was to call 'Daddy', I remember being singularly unimpressed by the fact that he had brought me a lovely pair of Egyptian sandals which turned out to be several sizes too small!)

The first days of the war actually provided the biggest problems for mothers about to give birth, for in the big cities which had been evacuated many of the

War or no war, romance would still go on. A picture to bring back nostalgic memories for anyone who was in love when war broke out.

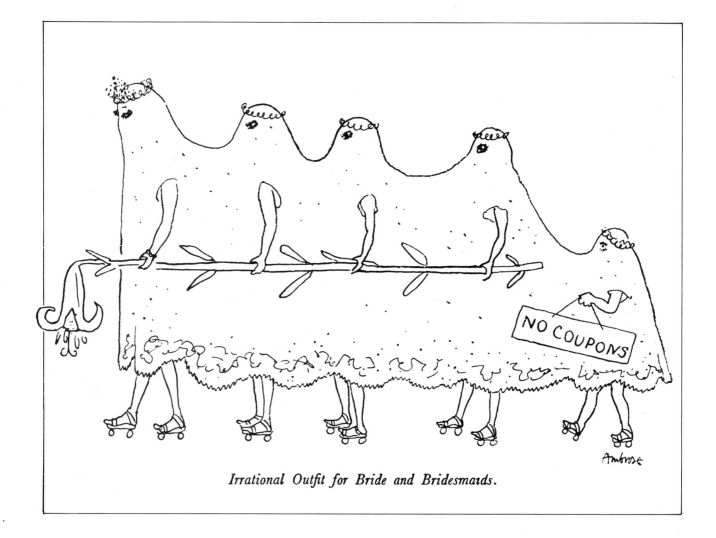

Irrational Outfit for Bride and Bridesmaids.

maternity clinics had been shut, and those which had been opened in the smaller country hospitals were unable to cope with the demand. There were private nursing homes throughout the country for those women who could afford them (the National Health Service had not yet been instituted), but in the main it was hard-pressed midwives who coped with the mounting number of births as best they could – though many a father or mother-in-law brought an infant into the world when help failed to arrive – and undoubtedly ante-natal care as a whole left much to be desired for many months of the war.

Pregnancy was not on every woman's mind at this time, however, and the pleasures of sex were now somewhat keener because of the uncertainty of the times – a fact which was reflected, if rather primly, in the women's magazines. A frequently voiced question from anxious and usually anonymous young ladies was whether they should sleep with their boyfriends. 'Why shouldn't we have this happiness before he goes away?' one reader asked *Woman* magazine. 'He says we may never see each other again and I know he loves me as dearly as I love him.'

The magazine's advice was both moral and stern.

A cartoonist's suggestion for the potential bride on how to dress herself and her bridesmaids in wartime Britain!

A page of early wartime weddings from The Lady *magazine, 21 September 1939.*

Weddings in Wartime

Left: The Hon. Basil Feilding, third son of the late Viscount and Viscountess Feilding, and Miss Rosemary Eardley-Wilmot, who were married quietly at Ascot last week

Below, left: Mr. K. V. Braddon and his bride, Miss Joyce Stuart Pearson, leaving St. John's Parish Church, Hampstead, after their wedding last week

Uniforms and Gas Masks

Right: The bridal couple leaving Brompton Oratory after the wedding of Flight-Lieutenant P. J. Sanders and Miss Welbergen

Left: Captain J. S. Dodd, son of Sir Robert and Lady Dodd, and Miss Audrey Johnson, of Prestwick, Manchester, who were married at St. Anne's Church, Eastbourne

Above: Special constables form a guard of honour at the wedding of Mr. G. P. Bartholomew and Miss Vivian Beresford, daughter of Frank Beresford, the artist

*One of a stark series of posters issued to combat the
danger of venereal disease.*

'This time of all times is not one for irresponsibility,' it replied. 'If he loves you as you say, your sweetheart will see the wisdom of patience. Remember, too, the emotions you speak of may well be the result of excitement and unnatural tension.'

Another equally torn young lady attempted to justify her decision to sleep with her boyfriend by declaring in a letter to *Woman's Own* that 'nine out of ten couples do this'. The journal's agony aunt responded brusquely that 'nine out of ten *don't*!' and insisted that anyone who anticipated the privileges of marriage at this time was 'an enemy to her country, which does not want to be faced with the further problems of unwanted children born out of wedlock'.

While there were certainly many young women wrestling with such ethical problems – and a good few succumbing to their lovers' advances, as the evidence of the increasing numbers of unmarried mothers as the war progressed bears witness – the nation's prostitutes certainly had no such reservations and enjoyed a time of unprecedented prosperity following the declaration of war.

If these girls had a problem, though, it was that of spotting and being spotted by customers in the blackout. The girls in the West End of London were the first to resolve the matter by carrying small torches in the pockets of their white mackintoshes and flashing these at intervals to indicate their presence. Even if spotted by a patrolling policeman or warden, the girls still had plenty of time to turn off the torch and disappear into the shadows before they were caught. (It has been suggested that this 'flashing' was the origin of the term now generally applied to men who expose themselves to women!)

The blackout also meant that the girls did not necessarily need to seek out alleyways to satisfy the needs of their clients; and members of the Mass Observation Unit who reported on conditions in London during the war in their magazine, *Us*, noted how shop doorways were now being used extensively for sex, and that even in busy high streets, 'the most unprecedented audacities were being achieved'. In surveying one particular street in Soho in September 1939, an observer of the Unit reported being accosted by over thirty women in the space of 120 yards – a number unequalled before and most probably not matched since!

In fact, the number of prostitutes everywhere rose sharply, although their ranks were undoubtedly augmented by 'part-timers', wives or girlfriends with husbands and lovers in the services, who supplemented their meagre finances by selling their bodies. The cover of the blackout also enabled these girls to avoid the unwelcome attentions of any pimps – whose numbers, conversely, had been considerably *depleted* through the calls of the armed forces!

The enforced gloom which covered city and town during the early days of the war obviously increased the possibilities for men to make advances to women, whether welcomed or not – a fact which was the subject of much ribald comment in music-hall and variety jokes. A favourite story of the autumn of 1939 concerned the man who had picked up a 'tart' (as prostitutes were widely called) and after having sex enquired how much he owed her.

'Half a crown', came the reply. (This sum is equivalent to just twelve and a half pence today.)

'That's rather little, isn't it?' the man said in obvious surprise. To which his companion replied: 'Well, I manage all right, what with my old age pension!'

A MAIDEN LOVED

AN IDLE WORD

A COMRADE LOST

AND ADOLF SERVED

Another poster warning of the dangers of promiscuity.

"NOW! WHERE'S THAT BLOKE HITLER !!"

16 Drink Up for Victory

To calm their nerves in the uncertain days of September 1939, the men and women of Britain naturally turned to their favourite relaxants, cigarettes and alcohol – or 'fags and booze' as they were popularly known. And it is a remarkable fact that while practically every institution in the British Isles was closed in the immediate aftermath of the declaration of war, only two remained constantly open throughout the entire period: the churches and . . . public houses!

The pre-war price of a pint of beer was 6d (two and a half pence), with a single whisky costing 9d (a bottle of Scotch retailed at around 15s), while popular brands of cigarette such as Woodbines, Capstan Navy Cut and Player's Number 3 (plain or 'cork-tipped') sold at prices ranging from 6d for a packet of ten, one shilling for twenty and just under three shillings for fifty. Within a few months of the war breaking out, however, these prices were to skyrocket following the inevitable shortages as supplies of tobacco, and sugar and grain for the breweries and distilleries, became increasingly difficult to obtain.

The ever-inventive 'man in the street' had soon devised a variation of the old song 'You Are My Sunshine' which was to be heard all over the country, illustrating this shortage and the craving for a cigarette:

'You are my sunshine,
My lovely Woodbine,
Please don't take my Woodbines away!'

Undoubtedly, though, in the first few days of September the public house was the only place where men and women could enjoy a drink or two and put the cares of the war behind them in convivial company. This was a situation that the landlords and brewers were naturally anxious to foster. 'Come to the pub tonight,' a September advertisement placed by the Brewers Society urged, 'and talk things over – over a glass of beer. The pub brings out the wisdom from a man because he can talk at ease there: he has a friendly audience. And there is the beer! The barley malt and hops in beer revive your spirits. Beer puts you in a cheerful, natural mood. It makes you yourself. That is why beer is best!'

A powerful advertisement for milk – though many people wanted something a little stronger!

'Guinness is good for wartime nerves' – according to this famous campaign which the brewing company inaugurated in September 1939.

A happy group of drinkers in a London pub putting thoughts of the war far from their minds.

One of the leading breweries, Whitbreads, underlined the message with a series of advertisements for its beer which read: 'Its rich strength will lift your hearts and renew those homely, happy smiles from which your daily fortitude is drawn.'

Later, when the fear of spies and informers gripped the country, publicans were encouraged to prevent careless talk in their bars and report any suspicious discussions or strangers asking unusual questions to the local police. But in September 1939 it was declared patriotic to visit the pub and 'Drink for Victory'!

In a powerfully worded argument, the *Brewers' Journal* declared, 'Sales of beer in this country yield the Chancellor of the Exchequer £256,000 a day. The daily cost of the war is £6,000,000, so that one Serviceman in twenty-four is being clothed, equipped, fed and paid out of the beer duty and one aircraft in twenty-four is also being built at the expense of the beer drinker. A man may spend far more money on new clothes or a wireless set and bring no grist to the financial mill . . . Beer drinkers are carrying the major burden of the cost of the war!'

In another essay in the *Morning Advertiser*, a commentator pointed out – somewhat tongue in cheek – that the entire cost of the war could be met if every adult drank half a bottle of whisky and smoked two packets of cigarettes a day!

Emotive words were similarly used by the *Wine and Spirit Trade Review* to encourage the consumption of wines and champagne. 'If the consumption of drink is cut down,' the *Review* argued, 'there would almost certainly be a resort to the use of drugs, with results too horrible to contemplate, and that would be only one form of vice that would follow. Even in war-time let us be sensible on this question.' (The fact that alcohol is itself a form of drug seems to have been completely overlooked in the argument!)

The various temperance organizations who were doing their best to steer the country away from drink found the suggestion of taking a glass or two anything but sensible, and would have no truck with claims from the wine trade that by consuming French wines we were putting much-needed money into the pockets of those who were lined up with us against the Nazi foe. One group, the National Temperance Federation, was soon demanding that pubs should be allowed to be open only five and a half hours a day, that *no* spirits should be sold from Friday to Sunday, and that both beer and spirits should be further diluted.

Such comments will doubtless evoke memories for many who were alive at the time, that beer certainly *seemed* more watery than it had done previously. Indeed, a popular joke related the conversation between a landlord and one of his customers.

Be careful what you say + where you say it!

CARELESS TALK COSTS LIVES

One of Fougasse's famous 'Careless Talk Costs Lives' posters warning about the dangers of letting drink run away with your tongue in a pub!

'It looks like rain,' the publican said, putting a pint down on the counter.

'Yes,' the customer replied, 'I didn't think it was beer.'

Regardless of the quality, the drinkers of Britain still *had* their pints in the autumn of 1939. But when the war really began to bite in the spring of 1941, it became an increasingly painful sight to find notices declaring 'No Beer' posted outside pubs and off-licences. Those premises that did open frequently rationed their regular customers while turning away strangers.

'It was not only the beer that became scarce,' Jack Montague, a former Manchester publican, recalled, 'but glasses were also in short supply, and there were some pubs I know that asked their customers to bring their own mugs! When things got really short, I used to only open up for a couple of hours in the evening, or maybe on alternate days. I still seemed to get just as many customers, though, and we were always packed.

'I remember there were always people trying to get you to sell them a bottle of Scotch or brandy from under the counter, offering to pay double the price or else give you other things in exchange that were in short supply like sugar and butter. It made my wife very frustrated when she heard what some of the customers were prepared to offer – but the fact was we rarely had spirits to sell.'

There were also campaigners who wanted to use the war as a reason for putting a stop to smoking in places like pubs, cinemas, cafés and even on public transport – but they were inevitably fighting a losing battle.

As the manufacturers battled to keep pace with demand while their stocks of tobacco leaf dwindled, their advertising increasingly urged smokers not to hoard, but instead cut down their consumption by a quarter. Cigarettes were certainly smoked down to the very end – pins often being used to get the last draw! The cigarette butt in ashtrays and squashed out on the floors and pavements also became a thing of the past, the more desperate smokers even crushing what little remained into the bowl of a pipe! Interestingly, pipe tobacco never became as difficult to find as cigarettes, a fact attributed by some disillusioned smokers to it being augmented by a variety of ingredients such as leaves and dried hay!

In such a shortage, suppliers will always emerge to make money out of hardship. 'Bootleg' whisky and gin were later to appear in some of the major cities of Britain, and resourceful importers somehow managed to get hold of strange brands of cigarettes from far-away places such as Turkey. Those who drank or smoked these offerings did so at a very real risk to their stomachs and lungs!

AN URGENT REQUEST **TO SMOKERS.**

EMPTY CIGARETTE AND TOBACCO CARTONS, CARDBOARD BOXES AND TINS.

Please hand these to your Tobacconist. By doing so you will help your Country · · · · ·

THIS ADVERTISEMENT IS ISSUED BY THE IMPERIAL TOBACCO COMPANY (OF GREAT BRITAIN & IRELAND), LTD

Not only had cigarettes themselves to be conserved in Britain, empty packets and tins were also saved to help in the war effort!

17 The Last Score for Sport

Sport in Britain came to a dramatic halt the day war broke out. It was an event unparalleled in the nation's history, and though most of the sporting associations had feared that the cancellation of some events was inevitable if the declaration were made, the result meant the end – for the time being at least – of what was then the country's biggest industry.

Although it is not possible to put a precise figure on the total involved (the sum of £40 million has been suggested), the amount of money being spent on betting alone in 1939 was more than that being spent in the largest staple industry – the building trade – and more than four times the nation's milk bill. And this is without taking into account entrance money for professional fixtures, the amounts spent on equipment for personal sports, and the other incalculable sums for travelling to venues, the purchase of programmes and souvenirs, and so on. September 3 was certainly a black day as far as everyone with a vested interest in sport was concerned.

Yet, until the very last moment, the nation's favourite sporting fixtures had carried on as if nothing could possibly change them. The closing games of an exciting cricket season were being played; the Football League fixtures were already under way; and the 'sport of kings', horse racing, was still drawing many thousands to the racecourses and uncounted millions into the betting shops. Individuals were still enthusiastically playing golf, tennis and bowls, though many did suspect that if the German bombers came their favourite links, courts and greens might soon be out of action.

Those sports which took place at night and depended on floodlighting had been immediate victims of the blackout – which meant the stopping of speedway and greyhound racing for six years, as well as making it extremely difficult to stage indoor ice hockey, snooker, all-in wrestling, boxing or table tennis.

What was to prove the last full Saturday sporting programme took place on 2 September and produced some memorable stories for the fans to chew over in the weeks that followed. For although a number of sports were again to be played in a month or so's time, the immediate impact of the war was to take away the cream of the professionals and no fixture would ever be quite the same until peace was once more restored.

In cricket, Yorkshire and Sussex completed a remarkable game at Hove, which the team from the north won by nine wickets. Such a score had seemed highly unlikely when Sussex had scored 387 in their first innings on their favourite ground – and indeed, Yorkshire managed to top this by only 5 runs, thanks to a magnificent 103 from Len Hutton. Yet, in their second innings, Sussex were scuttled out for just 33 runs, the Yorkshire bowler Hedley Verity taking seven wickets for just 9 runs. The visitors then scored the required 30 runs for victory at the cost of just one wicket: that of Hutton, who could manage only a single! (As a matter of record, though Verity was to finish top of the national bowling averages that year, Hutton had to be satisfied with second place in the batting table behind W. R. Hammond.)

Thereafter, there was to be no more first-class cricket in England until 1944 – such matches as did take place being played by scratch sides, mixing professionals and amateurs. For a time there was a fear that many of the best cricket grounds in the country might be ploughed up to make way for air-raid shelters, but an assurance to the contrary by the Ministry of Agriculture eased the apprehension.

Many football fans, however, were understandably anxious on that Saturday morning as to whether their favourite League teams would be playing. A notice in all the morning papers convinced them that matches *would* take place; but such was the general sense of apprehension that all gates were considerably down. The press release stated: 'The FA announce that a message has been received from the Home Office that the situation at the present time does not warrant today's matches being cancelled.'

Arsenal, the season's early pace-setters, were at home to Sunderland and drew the biggest crowd of the day at Highbury, just over 20,000. This was, though, less than half what they might have expected in better days for such an attractive fixture. As it was, Arsenal rewarded the fans who did turn up by winning 5–2, their famous centre-forward Ted Drake scoring four of these, and his striking partner, George Drury, getting the other. Hastings and Burbanks replied for Sunderland.

On the following day, Arsenal, like many other professional football clubs, urged their staff to join up, and a total of 42 players out of 44 promptly did so. The famous stadium itself became an ARP centre, and when the club did recommence playing fixtures with a reconstituted side, they temporarily shared the ground of their great rivals, Tottenham Hotspur, at White Hart Lane. (At the outbreak of the war, Tottenham

A dour-looking Len Hutton, who scored a century and a single in his two innings for Yorkshire in their last game before war broke out.

Tommy Lawton, the centre-forward of the then current League champions, Everton, who scored twice in the club's last game before war was declared. Lawton's goals resulted in a 2–2 draw with Blackburn Rovers.

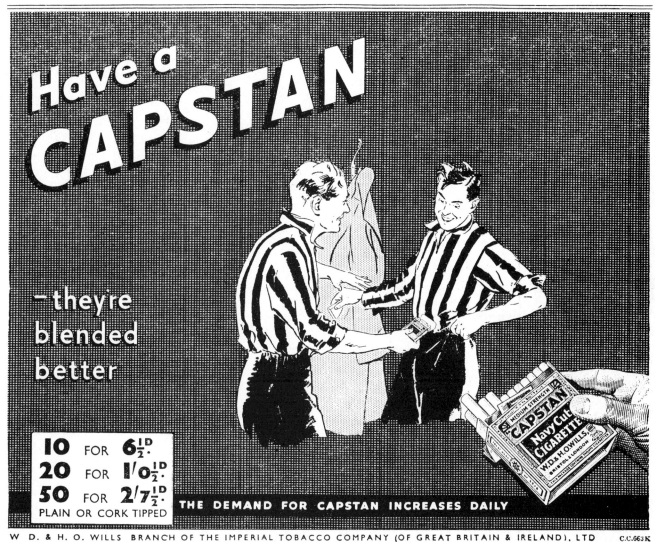

Have a CAPSTAN

– they're blended better

10	FOR	**6½**ᴰ.
20	FOR	**1/0½**ᴰ.
50	FOR	**2/7½**ᴰ.

PLAIN OR CORK TIPPED

THE DEMAND FOR CAPSTAN INCREASES DAILY

CAPSTAN Navy Cut CIGARETTE W.D.& H.O.WILLS

W D. & H. O. WILLS BRANCH OF THE IMPERIAL TOBACCO COMPANY (OF GREAT BRITAIN & IRELAND). LTD   C.C.663 K

were a Second Division side like those other famous Londoners, West Ham.)

Everton, the previous season's champions, drew 2–2 at Blackburn Rovers, with that other legendary centre-forward, Tommy Lawton, getting both the visiting team's goals. Liverpool scraped a 1–0 victory over Chelsea. Among other familiar footballing names then established as First Division sides – though no longer so – were Blackpool, Wolves, Grimsby and Brentford. In Scotland, Glasgow Rangers, who were then leading the table, were away at Third Lanark where they won 2–1 with goals by Thornton and Gilmour, while Celtic, in fifth place, were 1–0 winners at home against Clyde.

In fact, football fans everywhere – many of whom were soon to join the players they admired in the

Football used as a means of promoting cigarettes. An advertisement from 3 September 1939 – and some years ahead of its time in terms of the commercialization of sport.

services – mourned the premature end to the season. One of the most charitable decisions of that weekend came from Southampton where the Football Supporters' Club decided to offer all its available funds to the Government on loan and free of interest. The sum the club handed over was the not inconsiderable figure of £409.

It was not until 21 October that football resumed once again in Britain – for the time being on a regional basis, the professional clubs divided into eight local leagues in England and Wales and two in Scotland – though the scores which resulted from these 'friendlies' almost immediately revealed which clubs had been able to gain the release of their best players for fixtures and which had not. Queen's Park Rangers, for example, playing an Army side, won 10–2, while Norwich City put 18 goals past Brighton without a single reply! And although it is true to say that wartime football was enlivened by a whole new series of abusive remarks from the crowds directed at referees, such as 'Take your ruddy gas mask off!', the games were soon being viewed as a big anticlimax and gates were not the same again until peace-time.

From the Government's point of view this was not altogether unwelcome, because it had already been decided that fairly strict limits would have to be put on attendance figures to enable people to shelter in the ground or in the immediate vicinity if an air raid occurred. But it was equally true to say – as one national newspaper's football commentator did, sadly bemoaning the fact that he and his fellow scribes now had so little to write about – that sports such as football have a major effect on people's morale and a successful Saturday afternoon programme of matches would probably have done more to raise everyone's spirits than the campaign urging cheerfulness which the Government had just set in motion, at a cost of £50,000!

Britain's most popular form of betting, Football Pools, were immediate victims of the war. Although it would obviously have been difficult to administer them under the new conditions, the Government had actually taken the step of banning all Pools forms upon the outbreak of the war, ostensibly to save the hard-pressed Post Office work. The promoters, however, suddenly denied their income, began to lobby Parliament as soon as the regional leagues were formed, and the Government agreed to the setting-up of a single entity called Unity Pools which embraced all the pre-war companies of Littlewoods, Vernons, Copes, Shermans, etc. This was opened for business in November. The agreement was that part of the takings would go to war charities, and in order to save paper the forms were to be printed in the national newspapers. (Special instructions with these forms asked subscribers to ensure that they did not fill in their lines with 'blotty' ink as their entries might be subject to dispute and disqualification!)

Unity Pools undoubtedly lacked much of the glamour of peace-time pools – just as the game of football itself did – and the investment in them dropped sharply. For the punter there was really no guide to form as teams were subject to constant changes of players. More importantly, with fewer investors, the first dividends became much smaller. In the first three weeks of Unity Pools, for example, the winners of the Penny Pool won dividends of just £1500, £1073 and £750 – very small sums indeed in comparison with the huge pre-war prizes.

What big prize money there was to be won in the autumn of 1939 seemed more likely to come from horse racing which, though it was initially banned on 3 September, was back in full swing at Newmarket from the middle of October. However, fewer courses staged meetings during the ensuing six years, though attendances at these were often surprisingly large, and it was a matter of some controversy as to just where and how those who arrived in their cars had obtained their petrol. The fact that the winner of the last race to be run on Saturday 2 at Manchester had been a horse called 'Vain Fancy' was seen as very apposite by those who believed that the sport had no place being run at all in wartime Britain.

Many of the everyday sporting activities such as golf, tennis and bowls continued to be played throughout the war, though a large proportion of the venues disappeared to meet ARP needs, while equipment also became increasingly difficult to replace with manufacturers occupied in producing more necessary items. A large number of golf clubs was similarly requisitioned for military purposes (to the horror of their members watching the destruction of greens carefully brought to perfection by years of hard work!) and even those that escaped this fate were still required to set up anti-landing devices in case of invasion. The famous headquarters of tennis at Wimbledon became a decontamination centre, and many hard courts throughout the country proved ideal bases for gun batteries.

There were, however, those people who thought anyone spending time in sporting activity during a time of national emergency was being unpatriotic – though another lobby argued that if a man or woman could relax for a few hours from their war work without jeopardizing it in any way, they would surely return to their tasks refreshed and invigorated. But whichever viewpoint one took, there was no doubt that 3 September heralded one of the bleakest eras in sport in British history – an era which was not to end until 1947.

18 Animals Go to War

The British have long been a nation of pet-lovers and their favourite animals, birds, fish and other creatures were not forgotten at the outbreak of the war. The tragedy remains, though, that in people's concern for their pets, rather than see them subjected to the dangers of air raids or an agonizing death through gas poisoning, close to a million were destroyed throughout the whole country in the first week of September. (As support for this figure, in the Greater London area alone out of an estimated total of one million cats and 400,000 dogs, some four hundred thousand animals – chiefly cats – were painlessly destroyed in the first week of the war.)

Although in the light of what transpired in the following weeks, many pet owners had clearly acted too hastily, there could be no denying the humane thinking behind their actions. Arthur J. Hammond, who was a veterinary surgeon in Clapham between 1939 and the end of the war, recalled recently: 'You have to remember that at the start of the war everyone was frightened of being gassed. And a lot of people, especially the elderly, didn't want their pet dogs and cats to suffer, so they brought them along to the vets to be put down. Lots of families were evacuated, of course, and couldn't take their pets with them so the same thing happened.

'Those first few days of September were heartbreaking. I would find queues of people outside my surgery every morning. Sometimes children with a dog on a lead or a cat mewing in a cardboard box. A lot of them had tears running down their faces and none of them really wanted their pets to be destroyed. Some vets I know were so upset they just couldn't cope.

'I've no idea just how many I put down at that time, but I remember I had to keep some of the bodies in my coal cellar until they could be collected. Someone later told me that over 80,000 carcasses were buried one night during the first week of the war in a burial ground in the East End.'

Another factor which influenced this wholesale slaughter was a rumour which for a time gripped much of the country that it had been made compulsory to destroy pets in the event of war. A report in *The Times* of 7 September graphically details this under the heading 'Many Cats and Dogs Destroyed – No Truth in Rumour of Compulsion':

'A widespread and persistent rumour that it is now compulsory to get rid of domestic animals is causing many thousands to be taken for destruction, states the National ARP Animal Committee. As a result of this rumour, centres run by animal welfare societies (who are represented on the committee) are filled with the bodies of animals, and thousands more are being brought in every day.

'The committee emphasizes that there is no truth whatever in these rumours, and asks householders not to have their animals destroyed unless they are going away and cannot either take them with them or find anyone else to look after them. Apart from everything else, the huge destruction of cats that is continuing at present may lead to a very serious and even dangerous increase in vermin, such as occurred in Madrid and other Spanish cities through the same cause.'

The RSPCA was the biggest of these animal welfare societies to be inundated with desperate pet-lovers, and did its best to allay the panic. The Society had, in fact, been making preparations for the care of animals in wartime for several years. In the official report of its war work, *Animals Were There* (1947), the beginning of these preparations is fascinatingly described. In March 1936 the organization decided to send one of its senior representatives to meet an official of the newly formed air-raid precautions section of the Home Office to discuss animal casualties.

'Received with the traditional courtesy of the civil servant,' the report states, 'the representative nevertheless felt he was making little impression and was being regarded as just another of those cranks who are always bothering with animals. Indeed, it was not until the representative asked, "What are you going to do if half of the four thousand milk-float horses belonging to one firm in London become casualties?" that the civil servant began to really take notice. At this he exclaimed, "Really, the more one studies the subject of air-raid precautions, the more vast and complex does it seem to become." Thereafter, however slow to move the officials concerned might be, it could not be gainsaid that the situation had been brought home to them, though we must all share the blame for the lack of preparation which has so frequently characterized this country in its attitude to the likelihood of war.'

While the government department in question went laboriously about its work, the RSPCA itself wasted no time in preparing a booklet, *Air Raid Precautions for Animals*, which proved very popular with the public, running into six editions and selling over 100,000 copies by the time war broke out. Contained in the booklet were details of the 'Cat and Dog Grasper', an easily-made device consisting of a long pole with a running noose on the end for rescuing animals trapped amidst debris. It had been invented by one of the Society's inspectors after visiting the site of an explosion and finding great difficulty in pulling free some animals.

According to *Animals Were There*, there were a number of pet-lovers who believed the alternative to having their animals put down was to protect them with gas masks! If human beings could be supplied with

Many thousands of pets were put down in the immediate aftermath of the declaration of war on 3 September – though thanks to the dedicated work of organizations like the PDSA, a great number of others, such as this dog, were saved.

these to save themselves – these people argued – why shouldn't animals be treated the same?

'This created such a demand that the RSPCA had of necessity to warn the public that there was a growing exploitation in gas masks for animals,' the report says. 'Some types were useless, and one kind, made in Germany, with the object no doubt of gaining a little useful foreign exchange for the Fuehrer, was sold at £9! The mask was effective but involved the use of a special harness and was only suitable for very large dogs.

'As so frequently happens, the RSPCA had to intervene to prevent those who are devoted to animals from being defrauded. Nevertheless, one can but admire a working man who, when being shown one of these masks, produced a pound note to purchase it. On discovering that the figure was £9 he returned home for the remaining £8. Happily, he was in good hands, for, on his return, he was shown by the Society's officials how to protect his dog for an outlay of a few pence.'

A still more curious story of human devotion is related in the same report. 'Another enquirer,' it says, 'caused something of a diversion by asking if she could be supplied with gas masks for . . . bees! The harassed officials at first wondered if it were a joke. It was soon realized that the enquirer was animated by a genuine concern, but, on ascertaining that the hives were in open country, they were able to assure the enquirer that, although bees would no doubt be very sensitive to poison gas, it was unlikely that the enemy, with all his resources, could so saturate the air of the countryside as to harm the bees themselves!'

One further headache faced the RSPCA the

A whimsical David Langdon cartoon from Punch *showing that pets were every bit as much at war as their owners!*

weekend that war broke out. The report adds: 'London school children were being rapidly evacuated to the country and there was the immediate problem of hundreds of school pets to be faced. Once more the services of the Society were in demand to deal with those dogs, cats, rabbits, guinea-pigs and birds, to say nothing of three young alligators that one school had decided to adopt!'

In fact, an untimely end at the vet's was not the only peril that the nation's cats faced in September 1939 – for there were cat thieves about, too. A report in the *Daily Express* warned its readers: 'Watch your cats. Thieves have been busy in London since the war began stealing them – especially Persians. An animal welfare authority said yesterday that the thefts appear to be organized. There is a shortage of cat pelts in the fur trade.'

Nor was this the end of the story. For according to a report picked up by the Mass Observation Unit: 'A Hampstead charwoman told us, "You know what they're doing with all them cats that vanishes? They use the skins for lining British warms [an officer's thick overcoat], and they boil the fat down for margarine or something. They do say there is cats in pies!"'

For a good many pets, it was not until the air raids actually began that the even tenor of their existence was disturbed – though there was a little less on their plates when shortages of animal foods began to develop. Queues outside pet shops were soon as common as those to be seen outside grocers' premises, and tins of cat and dog food became scarcer than fresh fruit. There were, apparently, dark mutterings among some devoted dog owners that their pets were going short of horse meat because it was being diverted for human needs!

Calming words were again issued by another animal welfare society, according to the *News Chronicle* which headlined a report on 5 September 'Iron Rations for Dogs':

'An appeal to families laying in emergency supplies not to forget their dogs was issued by the National Canine Defence League to-day. The League suggests tinned foods with a meat content as suitable "iron rations" for dogs, and points out that wholemeal rusks are an ideal cereal as they will keep for a considerable time even if not in tins.'

Cats managed to augment their food with small rodents, though it may well have come as something of a shock when the new wartime regulations made it illegal for them to be given fresh milk! However, in recognition of their services in keeping down rats and mice in warehouses and temporarily closed shops, a dispensation that they might have 'limited quantities of dried milk' was given official sanction.

Cats, too, were destroyed in large numbers in the early days of September 1939 – though this was not the fate of this pet belonging to a group of Auxiliary Fire Service members in London.

The RSPCA had again anticipated this shortage of pet food, and many wartime pet owners had cause to be grateful to the Society's pamphlet *Feeding Dogs and Cats in Wartime*, with its tips on augmenting their animals' diets with potatoes, the leaves of cabbages, cauliflowers and other chopped greens, stale bread and oatmeal, all of which could be mixed with a gravy made from bones or scraps. The addition of sardine oil or some oil from fish trimmings was said – perhaps optimistically – by the RSPCA to make the vegetables acceptable to cats!

There was, of course, quite a large number of pet owners who decided to take their animals with them when they moved from the cities to the country, regardless of the risks of their pets finding it difficult to settle down or running away. And there was help at hand for these folk – as this advertisement placed in all the national newspapers on 4 September reveals: 'EVACUATION OF ANIMALS. Offers of help from car owners in the work of collecting and transporting animals to the country would be gratefully appreciated. Animal Defence Society, 15, St James's Place, S.W.1.'

Like their owners, in fact, the pets of Great Britain displayed the same resourcefulness to survive and adapt once the initial unhappy period of human over-reaction had passed. Thereafter, as ever, they remained the friend and comforter who would see many an owner through the dark days that were to come.

ZOO SNAKES KILLED

The poisonous snakes at the Royal Zoological Park, Edinburgh, were destroyed yesterday following the announcement of war. The lions, tigers and other animals are being kept alive at present.

From *The Scotsman*, 4 September 1939

19 The Pen and the Sword

A few days after the outbreak of the war, the novelist and playwright A. A. Milne, already a household favourite as a result of his Winnie-the-Pooh books, was asked what he proposed to do for relaxation at this tense period in time. 'Continue writing,' Milne replied, 'reading *War and Peace*, and, as in the last war, taking each day as it comes.'

The British love of a good book was sorely tested by the war – tested not just by the restrictions of the blackout making reading itself difficult, but also by the shortage of paper on which to print the books. Add to this the problems of running bookshops and maintaining the library service when staff were constantly being called away to the war, and it is a wonder that literature continued to thrive at all through those dark days.

The Mass Observation Unit, monitoring the first days of September, reported later: 'The immediate effect of war was a big slump in the number of people using libraries. Besides a large decline in book-borrowing (despite the blackout), there is a marked tendency for fiction to gain over non-fiction. This was in the first week of the war, when the individual was suffering from shock just as much as the institution.'

The observers of MOU also recorded another interesting fact: 'In all libraries, in London, Manchester, Liverpool, and elsewhere, librarians noted a steep increase in demand for books dealing with current affairs and the last war, books about modern Germany and (above all) Hitler's *Mein Kampf*. There was no noticeable increase in the demand for humorous fiction.'

Apart from the public libraries, Britain at this time had a number of circulating libraries, including the famous Boots Booklovers Library, where patrons paid to borrow the latest works of fiction. The writers of popular fiction for women were particularly in demand in these libraries, including Monica Dickens, Frances Parkinson Keyes, Angela Thirkell and E. M. Delafield. They also thrived on historical novels by writers such as Margaret Irwin, Georgette Heyer, Phyllis Bentley and Daphne du Maurier, though undoubtedly the most borrowed books of the wartime period were both by Americans: *Gone With the Wind* by Margaret Mitchell (1936) and *Forever Amber* by Kathleen Winsor, which was not actually published until 1944!

The publishing trade also reported an immediate effect on business that autumn month. Retired publisher Rupert Hart-Davis recalled recently: 'Quite simply no one knew what was going to happen. All our publishing plans changed day by day, and with only a few people in the office to handle the production of books and even fewer salesmen on the road to sell them, the situation was very uncertain. As far as business was concerned, all I really remember at the start of the war was that cheap reprints sold well and new books very badly because the trade was so nervous about what it stocked.'

An ever-present reminder of the books that were published in wartime are the copies still to be found in second-hand bookshops which display on their reverse title pages the figure of a lion atop an opened book on which are printed the words 'Book Production War Economy Standard', and below this the legend 'This book is produced in complete conformity with the authorised economy standards.' Though not aesthetically pleasing to the eye with their small type, narrow margins and chapters which run on – as well as cheaper paper now invariably browned – these editions at least enabled authors to publish their work and the book itself to survive.

Naturally enough, most British authors felt nervous about the future, though for some the war was to enhance their reputations. J. B. Priestley, the Yorkshire-born novelist and essayist who had won a wide following with *The Good Companions* (1929), was all ready to achieve a literary 'first' on 3 September when the war intervened. He had been commissioned by the BBC to write a novel specially for reading on the radio. Heralding this broadcast, *The Listener* stated in its issue of 31 August:

'Next Sunday there is due to take place an event which is not only a striking innovation in broadcasting but one which may well prove to be a landmark in English literature. On the evening of 3 September, Mr J. B. Priestley is to read at the microphone the first instalment of his new and unpublished novel, *Let the People Sing*. For the first time in the history of British broadcasting an author has been asked to write a full novel expressly for the needs of the microphone.'

And when J. B. Priestley himself was asked why he had undertaken this unusual commission, he replied, 'I believe that whatever the state of the world this autumn, this type of entertainment will be likely to carry on whereas the theatre may well be seriously affected by the international situation.'

In fact, the dramatic developments of that third day of September caused the reading of *Let the People Sing* to be postponed – but not cancelled, and a week later Priestley made a little bit of literary history when he read the novel to an audience which was undoubtedly

An outstanding cartoon by Norman Mansbridge from Lilliput, September 1939.

several times bigger than it might well have been in peace-time.

Apart from touring the country to report on Britain at war for both home and foreign newspapers, Priestley also wrote several novels on this theme which found a large readership, the best of them being *Blackout in Gresley* (1942) and *Daylight on Saturday* (1943) about life in an aircraft factory.

BOOKS FOR THE WAR

Following advice given or from prudence, most of us have laid in gear of some sort against what the future may bring. So far as I know, none has yet advised the laying-in of books against the long autumn and winter nights, for recreation and cheer, for guidance, counsel and consolation.

Movement, now, will be limited; amusement of many accustomed kinds has already ceased. All may read; all, still, have access to this treasury of the universe of the mind. The buying of books and the joining of libraries will certainly provide many helpful and forgetful hours, and may, possibly, help to prepare a peace, in which the world may again bring forth some intellectual fruit.

**John Masefield,
President, National Book Council,
6 September, 1939**

Among other leading literary figures, Graham Greene, who had scored a tremendous public success with *Brighton Rock* in 1938, followed this with a spy story, *The Ministry of Fear*, and *The Power and the Glory* which won the Hawthornden Prize in 1940. Evelyn Waugh, who had been a public favourite for rather longer, produced *Put Out More Flags* (1942) which graphically described the impact of evacuation on the English countryside, and then followed this with perhaps his best work, *Brideshead Revisited*, recently successfully adapted for television.

Nevil Shute, the former aeronautical designer who took to novel writing at the outset of the war, rapidly became one of its most popular novelists through his ability to mix fast-paced action with easily understood technical data. An early work about the impact of the war on an ordinary English family, *What Happened to the Corbetts*, struck a chord with many readers, and when he followed this with *Landfall*, *Pastoral* and *Most*

Secret, he established the reputation of being an outstanding story-teller which has kept his name a household word to this day. Also deserving of mention are C. S. Forester, who wrote several novels based on the war as well as continuing his famous 'Hornblower' saga, and Hammond Innes, whose highly successful career got off to a fine start with *Wreckers Must Breathe* and *Attack Alarm*.

Those who continued to urge the public to read as a form of escapism – in particular politicians, churchmen, radio pundits and newspaper critics – almost without exception promoted the classic writers such as Jane Austen, Thomas Hardy and Charles Dickens, especially for the glimpses they provided of a happier and more peaceful world; though for a time, when the country's sympathies were being encouraged towards Russia, Tolstoy's *War and Peace* became the favourite bed-time reading for a great many people!

Clement Attlee, the leader of the Labour Party, was one who urged the reading of books, 'preferably English classics: Jane Austen is very soothing', he said. Canon Alexander of St Paul's Cathedral admitted, 'My refuge is Shakespeare'; while Mrs Bramwell Booth of the Salvation Army said, 'The book of books to me for sixty years past has proved the book for the moment, bringing just the word of authority, guidance and comfort. I suggest that in these days of dark evenings the *Bible* should be read aloud in the family group.'

Viewed with hindsight, one book most perfectly captured England in the opening days of the war: *The Oaken Heart*, written by the social historian and mystery-story writer Margery Allingham. Born in London in 1904, she grew up in Essex, and had her first book *Blackerchief Dick*, about smuggling and piracy on the Essex marshes, published when she was just a teenager. Much of Margery's life was to be spent in the rather remote Essex coastal village of Tolleshunt d'Arcy, and it was the events which occurred here that formed the background to *The Oaken Heart*, which was first published in 1941 and rapidly ran into several editions. Today, sadly, copies are hard to come by.

In *The Oaken Heart*, Tolleshunt d'Arcy is renamed Auburn, and the book takes the form of a long descriptive essay to an American describing the impact of war on this English backwater. It is, though, in many ways a

The writer and broadcaster J. B. Priestley, who became famous during the war, photographed here with Gracie Fields. This picture was actually taken by Basil Dean, the founder of ENSA.

Evelyn Waugh's book Put Out More Flags, *describing the impact of the evacuation on the countryside of Britain, earned further prestige for the author, seen here with his wife.*

microcosm of England as a whole, as I am sure this extract from Chapter Nine about 3 September will vividly demonstrate.

'At eleven o'clock the next morning Mr Chamberlain made his famous speech and, still like the family solicitor, so kindly and so very upset, told us it had come. We were at war. Still there was no band, no cheering, no noise; only this breathless feeling of mingled relief and intolerable grief. Poor Mother Peace was dead at last after all her sufferings.

'Grog and P.Y.C. were in the Post Office alone. They would not leave the phone. They were convinced that the great raids, with gas and everything else, would start on London and Paris the instant the German Government received the declaration, and that our raid on Berlin would begin the moment a Nazi plane crossed our coastline.

'I went into the garden and sat under the laburnum and the fancy red oaks. I could smell the sea, and I watched the sky over the rookery in the Vicarage elms, more than half expecting that I should suddenly see the warplanes coming like starlings in the spring, making the sky black. If the boys were right, they were just about due.

'I thought: "Well, it's come; this is the terminus. This is the explanation of the extraordinary sense of apprehension, of the unaccountable nostalgic sadness of the last few years. This is where our philosophy led. This is what was in the bag for all of us. This is what has come of curbing our natural bossiness out of deference to the criticism of the sophisticated cleversides of three continents. This is what comes of putting up with wrong'uns. This is what comes of not interfering when you see something horrible happening, even if it isn't your business. This is where we've been going. This was our portion after all."

'Then another thought came into my mind with the vehemence of a command. "Whatever happens, *whatever* happens, never go on pretending that things were going well before the war. Never deceive yourself that you could not foresee a dead end." I knew what I meant, although I had not been able to nail it down before. There had been a growing sense of dissatisfaction (none of it acute) in most of our generation for some time. Following the logical conclusions of our early disillusions, most of us were arriving at full maturity without a faith and without a hobby – two rather serious deficiencies in the adult. Some revolutionary change of popular interest had been indicated for some time. Now we certainly seemed to be going to get it, although it seemed criminally silly that we should have to find it in another war.

'I took another look at the sky over the estuary. It was as empty as the future.'

First published in 1939, The Black-Out Book featured George Bernard Shaw along with other famous personalities.

Strictly Personal

No. 25. George Bernard Shaw
When our elders talk of Shaw,
Echo rudely answers : " Pshaw ! "

Jerome said about Shaw . . .

BERNARD SHAW'S name first became familiar to the general public as the result of scurrilous attacks, disguised as interviews, made upon him by a section of the London evening press. The interviewer would force his way into Shaw's modest apartment, apparently for no other purpose than to bully and insult him.

Many people maintained that Shaw must be an imaginary personage. Why did he stand it ? Why didn't he kick the interviewer downstairs ? Failing that, why didn't he call in the police ? It seemed difficult to believe in the existence of a being so Christian as this poor, persecuted Shaw appeared to be. Every one talked about him.

As a matter of fact, the interviews were written by Shaw himself.

164   **THE BLACK-OUT BOOK**

Bright Thoughts from Evacuees

With evidences of evacuation on all sides the " Black-Out Book " presents a distilled selection of schoolboy howlers. Why, by the way, are howlers always

' Evacuation ' is what the sun does to water.

★

Hell hath no fury like a woman's corn.

★

A horticulturalist is a man of culture who spoils himself by being haughty.

★

A passive verb is one in which the subject is the sufferer, such as " He was married to her."

The future tense of " He is drinking " is " He is drunk."

★

" Courting disaster " means when a man gets engaged.

★

Giraffes and ostriches need long necks because their heads are so far from their bodies.

★

I think Parnell was wrong and Gladstone was right. I have no reason for saying this.

★

No one has yet succeeded in spitting an atom.

★

Cæsar was warned to be careful of the Ideas of Frederic March.

★

Crops grow best where the ground is futile.

The Buffalo was invented to stop trains.

The Things that Teachers hear

attributed to boys? Do girls never blunder? For further examples of juvenile wit, the reader is referred to the collections of Mr Cecil Hunt.

A *pas seul* is something wrapped up in brown paper and string.

*

A panorama is a sort of hat worn in South America.

Moral

A youth should not be made to hate study before he know the causes to love it : or taste the bitterness before the sweet ; but called on, and allured, entreated and praised : Yea, when he deserves it not.

BEN JONSON

" Arguing in a circle " means a round-table conference.

*

An antiquarian is a man who drinks nothing but water.

A Republican is the same as a sinner.

*

A blue stocking is something mother uses to make clothes whiter.

*

Life insurance was first introduced in order to pay funeral expenses.

*

A Bison is something to be sick into.

20 Insuring the Future

'In view of the outbreak of hostilities,' a report in *The Times* of Saturday 2 September stated, 'the members of the Life Officers' Association and of the Associated Scottish Life Offices have been recommended to cease from issuing unrestricted new life policies at the rates of premium hitherto current.'

On first reflection it might be imagined that the onset of war would have quickly led to an impoverished country and a starving people – the traditional view of the impact of warfare on most nations. In fact, though the war was to cost Britain £6 million per day in the first few months (rising to a high of £13 million in the winter of 1944), it actually led to a period of prosperity for many sections of the population because of the extra work suddenly available for both men and women. From those early September days, many a household in the country had incomes not only from a husband but probably also from a wife and a son or daughter not in the services and employed in one of the reserved occupations.

Servicemen's families were undeniably the worst off, though the middle classes also suffered a substantial drop in their standard of living. Many lost their servants to the armed forces and had to sacrifice the regular refurbishment of their wardrobes. For the working classes, a decided improvement occurred when they were switched in great numbers from their more mundane peace-time occupations to the war effort and found themselves being much better paid. A building worker, for instance, on £2 5s in August 1939 might well have doubled this by September working in a munitions factory. For Mr Average, in fact, his pre-war wage of £2 17s 6d a week was to rise to around £4, while the figure for women rose similarly from 35 shillings a week to £2 15.

Money, in fact, was as much a concern to everyone in wartime as it had been in peace. Yet what occurred to the nation's finances was not always what might have been expected.

That graph of the world of finance, the stock market, remained 'stoic' in the week preceding the declaration of war, according to one commentator. The Stock Exchange itself was closed from Monday 4 September until Thurday 7, although inter-office dealings did continue unofficially among brokers strolling about Throgmorton Street on the Tuesday and Wednesday. When not preoccupied, these men could afford a smile at headlines in some of the popular newspapers declaring in inch-high letters: 'WILD BUYING ON WALL STREET: War Profits Expected!'

In fact, there was no wild speculation when the London Exchange re-opened, and there was widespread admiration for the smoothness of the transition of the market from peace-time to war. Although various con-

London prepares for attack from the skies. Many families filled sandbags and dug trenches to protect their homes, while for others there was always insurance cover!

MONEY
on active service

THE TASK OF THOSE RESPONSIBLE FOR THE CONTROL and conservation of great financial resources is not easy. Upon them will depend much of the Nation's ability to readjust industry and commerce at the end of the war. In the meantime, an urgent duty falls to every Director, Trustee or Member of a Committee responsible for the investment and employment of money. The Nation needs the use of vast sums *now*, raised in the form of five to seven-year Bonds—National War Bonds 1945-47.

By giving their unhesitating support and exerting fully their powers and influence now, the Nation's leading men of business can do immense service to the Country.

2½% National War Bonds
(1945-47)

A full Trustee Security — Price of issue £100 per cent — Subscriptions of £100 or multiples of £100 will be received until further notice—Interest accrues from date of purchase—Prospectus and application forms obtainable from Banks or Stockbrokers.

Issued by The National Savings Committee, London

trols and regulations had been brought into effect by the Government, the nation's financial machinery was clearly still functioning productively.

A financial columnist in the *New Statesman* with the perhaps singularly inappropriate name of 'Dives' had these reflective comments to make in the issue of 9 September under the heading 'Steady Markets':

'Although the Stock Exchange remained closed until Thursday, the trend disclosed by inter-office dealings on Tuesday and Wednesday was quietly steady. Gilt-edged, generally speaking, were put back to their minimum prices, but there was practically no liquidation; and among equities movements were small, buyers and sellers being fairly evenly balanced.

'At around £4, the £1 Sterling was regarded as having reached a level at which there should be no difficulty in holding it. Foreigners with Sterling balances in London are showing no disposition to withdraw funds, and the authorities are clearly gaining substantial holdings of gold and foreign exchange from British subjects now required to turn in these assets.'

Switching his attention to share prices in general, 'Dives' had this to say: 'Very broadly, shares of companies in the unessential trades (from the war standpoint), such as high class stores, motor manufacturers and cinemas have fallen. So, too, have tobaccos, on fears of dearer leaf resulting from the depreciation of Sterling, and even shares such as Woolworths and Marks & Spencers on fears of higher costs and moderately reduced sales. On the other hand, there has been a keen demand for shipping shares, which, it seems clear, must benefit from a rise in freights; for Argentine rails and a wide range of commodity shares covering rubbers, coppers, tin and lead-zinc issues. Higher commodity quotas already provide a logical basis for this movement. Another group which was bound to benefit from war conditions was American shares, which have risen quite spectacularly, much to the dismay of London "bears" and to the satisfaction of the "bull" speculators and the investment holders on this side of the Atlantic.'

Concluding his report, 'Dives' felt that a war budget from the Chancellor of the Exchequer, Sir John Simon, was inevitable. (It came, in fact, on 27 September,

increasing the standard rate of income tax from 5s 6d in the pound to 7s 6d and hammered those traditional favourites of all Chancellors, beer, spirits, wines and tobacco – plus sugar – as well as, controversially, reducing the income tax allowance for children: 'Now You *Know* There is a War On!' the *Daily Mirror* headlined its front-page report.) But the columnist still saw positive signs for the future and reckoned that with the nation's gold stocks and foreign resources now standing well in excess of £1 billion, the nation had 'a very formidable war chest'.

THE PROFITS OF WAR

In an excited market, all too reminiscent of the 'war babies' markets of generations ago, speculators from all over the US and some European neutral countries rushed to buy shares in steel, copper, sugar, aeroplanes, chemicals and shipping companies – of any and all industrial concerns that seemed likely to profit by war.

Prices rose by as much as 10 to 12 points in a number of issues, and though there was some profit-taking and some tentative short selling in late dealings, the general level at the close was but little below the best of the day.

At the close, the Dow Jones average for 30 industrial stocks showed a gain of 9.02 points. The railways average, however, was up only 2.65 points and the utilities average only one-third of a point.

From the *New York Times*, 5 September 1939

Money quickly became an important element in the fight against Hitler, and National Savings, which were enthusiastically supported right from the beginning of hostilities, played a significant role in the war effort.

The banks did not re-open in Britain until Tuesday 5 September although the National Safe Deposit in Westminster was in business bright and early from first thing on Monday morning to cope with the large queues of people wanting to put their most treasured possessions into its vaults. Those with cash in their pockets (and this included children as well as adults) soon became the subject of an intense campaign to help the war effort by buying National Savings Certificates, urged on by posters emblazoned with the slogan 'Lend to Defend the Right to be Free'. More effective still was the evil-looking cartoon insect called the 'Squanderbug' who became part of the campaign to warn people away from extravagance – buying things for the sake of buying them – but undoubtedly his sinister appearance gave many young children nightmares! (As

REGISTER
NOW FOR
COOKING FATS

FROM next Monday, July 22nd, Margarine and Cooking Fats will be rationed. You must now fill in the particulars on the 'Cooking Fats' page of your Ration Book, and also inside the front cover. Then take the Book to a retailer *immediately* for registration.

BUTTER & MARGARINE

With the coupons marked 'BUTTER & MARGARINE' you will be able to buy a total weekly ration of 6 oz. You can buy *all* butter or *all* margarine, or some of each. *If you are registered for butter* you need not register for margarine, as you will use the same coupons as for butter.

COOKING FATS
(or extra Margarine)

With the coupons marked 'COOKING FATS' you can buy 2 oz. per week of lard or compound lard, or, if you wish, 2 oz. of margarine. (This is in addition to any margarine you buy with your 'Butter & Margarine' coupons.) Dripping and suet are not to be rationed at present.

TEA

Tea is now rationed (2 oz. per week). You may buy from any shop you like — no registration is necessary. To avoid small quantities you may buy one week in advance. Make sure that your shopkeeper takes the coupons from the first page of SPARE Coupons (coloured buff) next to the SUGAR page.

ISSUED BY THE MINISTRY OF FOOD, GT. WESTMINSTER HOUSE, S.W.I

Queues of housewives hoping to buy precious food supplies became an everyday sight.

a matter of record, there are still several million pounds of unclaimed money remaining from wartime savings held in the Treasury's Consolidated Fund – where they will doubtless remain for another fifty years and more.)

For the man and woman in the street, however, it was the worries about rising prices and a run on food supplies that most concerned them in the early days of September 1939. Retail trade figures for this time clearly indicate a big increase in spending on food, clothing and other items – specifically for evacuation and the blackout – in the first month of the war: a whole 11 per cent up on the previous month, in fact. This despite government appeals to people not to buy any food beyond their usual weekly supply.

Among those most affected by this upsurge in public spending were, of course, shopkeepers, and John Morrison, who ran a grocer's shop in Peckham throughout the war, recalls: 'There were some who panicked, of course, and tried to buy up stocks of everything. We had to be very careful not to upset our regular customers and keep an eye out for the scroungers who were going round from one shop to another getting hold of as much as they could.

'Most people who came in wanted butter and bacon which were scarce, but *everyone* wanted sugar, and I just had to ration it. One day this woman I had never seen before came in to the shop and asked for six pounds. I said she could only have one and she went away complaining. When she came back later obviously having got the same reply at other grocers' shops and said she would have the one bag after all, I told her, "You can't, I've sold it!" What I don't think most people realized was that we were being rationed ourselves by our suppliers, so there was hardly enough to go round to begin with!'

Mr Morrison remembers that he would even get people coming to his shop who lived in the richer parts of London. 'They were the worst,' he says. 'They would arrive in their cars – some even had chauffeurs – and would try to load them up with everything we had. They were trying to take the poorer people's food: real parasites.'

From the other side of the counter, though, there were customers who thought the shopkeepers were taking advantage of the new circumstances and either deliberately keeping some items in short supply or else inflating prices. 'The Government keep telling us that there is plenty of food for everyone,' a Liverpool housewife, Joan Murphy, was quoted as saying in the second week of September, 'but you tell me which shops it's in. And even when you do find what you want, the price has gone up. The shopkeepers tell us they're being ruined by the war, but I think some of them are profiteering. I think a proper kind of official rationing should be brought in.' (And, of course, in January 1940, it was.)

Because of the rising cost of living, and despite the improved wages available in many of the new wartime jobs, public opinion continued to run high about the discrepancies in salaries. A Ministry of Labour report showed that while over two million people had received increases totalling £300,000 per week, some 330,000 folk had ended up with a net decrease of £26,000. A partial redress of this imbalance was achieved in the winter when wage increases of close to 10 per cent were awarded to almost three million people.

One fascinating sidelight on the topic of money occurred at this time when the *Daily Telegraph* published a revealing article about the fortunes being amassed by the German leaders. If anyone in Britain were to be accused of feathering their own nest as a result of the hostilities, said the paper, their efforts surely paled into insignificance when compared with the Nazi leaders, most of whom had started with nothing and in the space of a few years had become millionaires busy salting away their ill-gotten gains abroad. Among those the *Telegraph* named were:

'Ribbentrop: Foreign Minister, ex-Ambassador in London, has £1,948,000 in cash and securities and life insurance policies. Of this £633,000 is in cash.

Goebbels: Propaganda Minister, has £1,798,000 of which £927,000 is held in cash.

Goering: Field Marshal, has £1,501,400, of which £449,000 is in cash and securities.

Hess: Deputy Leader, has £1,108,500 of which £449,000 is in cash and negotiable paper.'

As to Hitler's fortune, the paper said it had no information, although it added with mischievous good humour, 'Whether the Fuehrer knows that his helpers have been preparing for bad weather is unknown!' Fifty years later, we do know just how bad that weather was ultimately to become for every one of them!

Postscript: The End of the Beginning

'Astonishment was world-wide when Hitler's crashing onslaught upon Poland and the declaration of war upon Germany by Britain and France were followed only by a prolonged and oppressive pause. Mr Chamberlain in a private letter published by his biographer described this phase as the "Twilight War". No air action, except reconnaissance, was taken against Britain; nor was any air attack made upon France by the Germans. The French Government requested us to abstain from air attack on Germany, stating that it would provoke retaliation upon their war factories, which were unprotected. We contented ourselves with dropping pamphlets to rouse the Germans to a higher morality. This strange phase of the war on land and in the air astounded everyone.

'Then, in May 1940, at last the slowly-gathered, long-pent-up fury of the storm broke upon us. Four or five millions of men met each other in the first shock of the most merciless of all the wars of which record has been kept. Within a week the front in France, behind which we had been accustomed to dwell through the hard years of the former war and the opening phase of this, was to be irretrievably broken. Within three weeks the long-famed French Army was to collapse in rout and ruin, and our only British Army to be hurled into the sea with all its equipment lost. Within six weeks we were to find ourselves alone, almost disarmed, with triumphant Germany and Italy at our throats, with the whole of Europe open to Hitler's power, and Japan glowering on the other side of the globe. It was amid these facts and looming prospects that I entered upon my duties as Prime Minister and Minister of Defence and addressed myself to the first task of forming a Government of all parties to conduct His Majesty's business at home and abroad by whatever means might be deemed best suited to the national interest.

'Our fate now depended upon victory in the air. The German leaders had recognized that all their plans for the invasion of Britain depended on winning air supremacy above the Channel and the chosen landing-places on our south coast. The preparation of the embarkation ports, the assembly of the transports, the mine-sweeping of the passages, and the laying of new minefields were impossible without protection from British air attack. For the actual crossing and landings complete mastery of the air over the transports and the beaches was the decisive condition. The result therefore turned upon the destruction of the Royal Air Force and the system of airfields between London and the sea. We now know that Hitler said to Admiral Raeder on July 31: "If after eight days of intensive air war the Luftwaffe has not achieved considerable destruction of the enemy's Air Force, harbours and naval forces, the operation will have to be put off till May 1941." This was the battle that had now to be fought.'

Winston Churchill

The indomitable spirit of wartime Britain personified!

ACKNOWLEDGEMENTS

The author is grateful to a great many people for their help in the writing of this book, and the majority of these are acknowledged in the text. However, he would also like to especially thank W. O. G. Lofts for his invaluable assistance with research; Sheila Coe of *The Box of Delights* in Skipton, North Yorkshire for providing contemporary artifacts and leaflets; Michael Moody and Jenny Wood of the Imperial War Museum also for contemporary material; and Alan Wilson, Colin Wright, Jane Clements, Miles Benjamin and Helen O'Malley for additional research material. I also received much help and assistance from the Houses of Parliament Archives, the Mass Observation Unit Archives, the BBC Sound Archives, and the staffs of The British Museum, The British Museum Newspaper Library and The London Library. The following publications have allowed me to quote from their pages covering September 1939: *The New Statesman*, *The Spectator*, *The Listener*, *The Countryman*, *The Times*, *The Daily Telegraph*, *The Sunday Express*, *The Lady*, *Radio Times*, *Daily Express*, *Time & Tide*, *Daily Mail*, *Daily Mirror*, *Punch*, *Variety* and the *New York Times*. Photographs have been supplied by the Imperial War Museum, Popperfoto, Keystone Press, Reuters and from the albums of my family and friends. I am grateful to each and every one of these people and organizations for without their help this book would not have been possible.

PETER HAINING

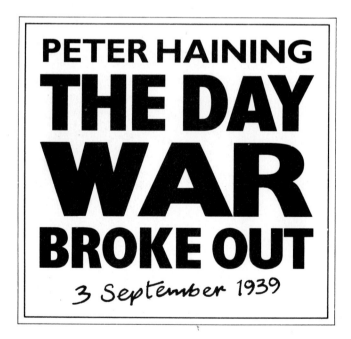

PETER HAINING
THE DAY
WAR
BROKE OUT
3 September 1939